CRITICAL THINKING, LOGIC & PROBLEM SOLVING

The Ultimate Guide to Better Thinking, Systematic Problem Solving and Making Impeccable Decisions with Secret Tips to Detect Logical Fallacies

by

BIGROCKS THINKING

Empower Up

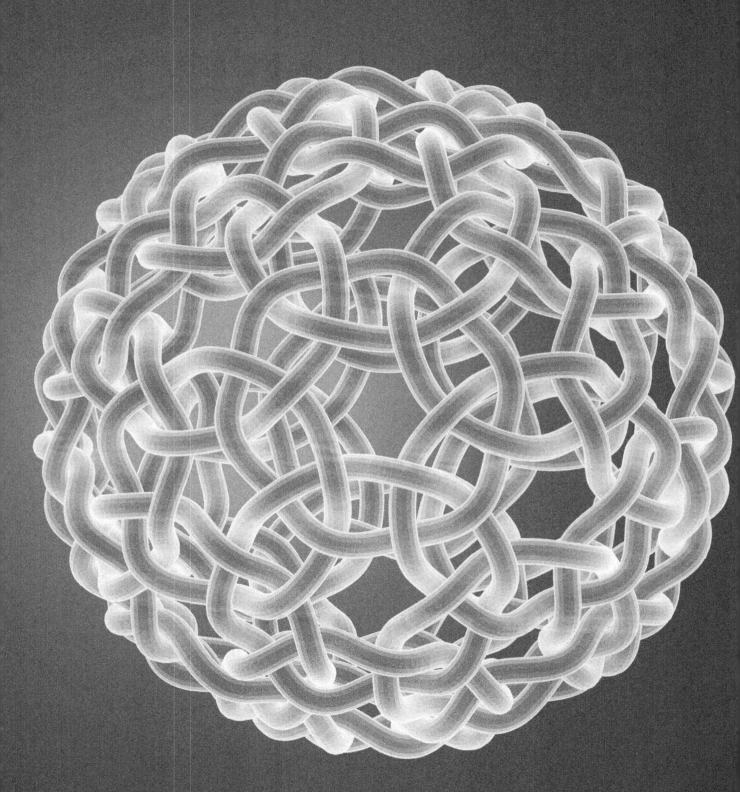

Contents

|Part 1| Critical Thinking 7

    Section 1: What Is Critical Thinking? 7

    Section 2: Skills You Need for Critical Thinking.. 9

    Section 3: The Barriers to Critical Thinking 11

    Section 4: Asking The Right Questions as a Critical Thinker 13

    Section 5: Paul-Elder Critical Thinking Framework 16

    Section 6: Fallacies 19

    Section 7: Cognitive Biases.. 22

    Section 8: Key Habits to Adopt to Improve Your Critical Thinking 24

    Section 9: Deductive vs. Inductive Reasoning 25

    Section 10: The Importance of Patterns 29

    Section 11: Understanding Causation and Correlation 32

    Section 12: The 8 Habits of Effective Critical Thinkers 34

    Section 13: Key Critical Thinking Steps 35

    Section 14: Exercises to Develop Critical Thinking 37

    Section 15: Useful Apps.. 39

    Section 16: The Relation Between Emotions and Critical Thinking 40

|Part 2| Logic, Structuring, & Framing 43

    Section 1: 5W2H Analysis to Describe a Problem (Who, What, Where, When, How, How Much)...... 43

    Section 2: SCQH—A Framework for Defining Problems and Hypotheses 49

    Section 3: MECE Principle & Synthesis 53

    Section 4: The 80/20 Rule 60

    Section 5: Top-Down and Bottom-Up Approach... 63

    Section 6: Logic/Issue Trees (Defining Structures, Grouping, and Logical Orders) 65

    Section 7: Logic Flow Trees, Decision Trees, and Yes/No Trees 77

|Part 3| Problem-Solving 81

    Section 1: Problem-Solving Definition and Process... 81

    Section 2: Pros and Cons Assessment 84

    Section 3: Prioritization Matrices 85

    Section 4: Decision Matrix 89

    Section 5: Organizing Action With the 5W2H Method 92

    Section 6: RACI Matrix 93

    Section 7: How to Leverage Constraints to Be More Creative 94

|Part 4| Achieving Clear and Effective Communication 97

    Section 1: Organizing Your Communication and Storytelling Techniques........................ 97

    Section 2: The Pyramid Principle.. 100

    Section 3: Ways to Structure Your Story 102

Section 4: Story Frameworks for Better Storytelling 105

Section 5: The End 108

How to Access Your Bonuses..109

How Can You Get the Best Out of This Book..109

|Part 1| Critical Thinking

Section 1: What Is Critical Thinking?

There are numerous definitions of critical thinking from various schools of thought. The intrinsic capacity to process and interact analytically with incoming knowledge could be one. This interaction is accomplished by making observations and logically connecting disparate pieces of information. Critical thinking can also be referred as the ability to interpret information factually and reach a sound conclusion. It entails the assessment of informational materials like statistics, facts, observable phenomena, and research findings.

To solve problems or make decisions, good critical thinkers can infer acceptable conclusions from a collection of facts and distinguish between relevant and irrelevant elements.

When you use critical thinking, you analyze, interpret, evaluate, and form opinions about what you read, hear, say, or write. The Greek word *kritikos*, which means "able to judge or distinguish," is where the word "critical" originates. Making trustworthy decisions based on trustworthy information is a key component of critical thinking.

Using critical thinking does not necessitate being pessimistic or fixating on flaws. It entails being able to focus your thoughts to dissect a situation or a piece of information, interpret it, and then use that interpretation to make a wise choice or judgment.

Although no one is born with a critical thinking mindset, people who continuously use it are said to have one. These are qualities that can be acquired and enhanced with use and practice. Curious and reflective individuals are critical thinkers. They delve deeper and ask more questions to learn more and look for answers. They analyze claims and arguments, distinguish between facts and opinions, and pose significant questions. They are open to questioning their views and have humility that enables them to acknowledge ignorance or a lack of understanding when necessary. Critical thinkers are flexible in their thinking. They actively enjoy learning and regard the search for new information as a lifetime endeavor, which is maybe the most important quality in a critical thinker.

You will articulate yourself more effectively, read more critically, and efficiently gather crucial information if you can think critically. You become a better thinker and problem solver with critical thinking. Critical thinking is amplified by the following three fundamental abilities:

1. **Curiosity** is the drive to find out more information, gather proof, and be receptive to novel concepts.
2. **Skepticism** entails not mindlessly trusting everything that you hear and having healthy skepticism about new information.
3. **Humility** is acknowledging that your beliefs are mistaken in the face of fresh, compelling evidence to the contrary.

Critical Thinking Examples

The situations that necessitate critical thinking vary by industry. Several instances include the following:

- A triage nurse evaluates the cases at hand and determines the treatment priorities.
- A plumber assesses the materials that would be most appropriate for a job.
- An attorney examines the evidence and develops a plan to win the case or determine whether to settle outside court.

- A manager examines customer feedback forms and uses the data to create a training session for staff members on customer service.

In essence, critical thinking calls for the use of reasoning skills. Being an active learner instead of a passive taker of information is key. Critical thinkers fiercely contest ideas and presumptions rather than taking them at face value. They are always open to learning that the assumptions, reasons, and conclusions do not accurately reflect the circumstance. Critical thinkers will identify, examine, and resolve issues methodically rather than solely depending on intuition or gut feelings.

What Exactly Does It Mean to Think Critically?

Critical thinking is a means of looking at things to determine the truth in a situation. It is based on evidence, observation, and reasoning. Determining the optimal course of action requires the capacity to look at a situation from various angles. The father of contemporary critical thinking is John Dewey.

According to him, critical thinking entails "active, persistent, and careful consideration of a belief or supposed form of knowledge in the light of grounds which support it and further conclusions to which it tends." Even though he wrote those remarks in 1909, the necessity for a logical approach to decision-making still exists today.

An individual with critical thinking abilities can:

- Distinguish between fact and opinion;
- Recognize the connections between concepts;
- Examine various viewpoints;
- Recognize the goals of others;
- Investigate the reasons for and against a position;
- Consider how their presumptions, ideas, and values are justified;
- Remain conscious of their thoughts;
- Analyze the significance and applicability of arguments and concepts;
- Recognize, construct, and evaluate arguments;
- Identify logical contradictions and mistakes;
- Methodically and consistently approach issues;
- Avoid jumping to conclusions too soon; and
- Adjust expectations in light of new information.

Top Things to Do Right Now to Improve Your Critical Thinking

Recognize Assumptions: Assumptions are something we all make, often without even realizing it. Consider what assumptions are pertinent to your issue, separate fact from opinion, and look for opposing stances.

Argument Evaluation: Analyze claims critically and assess them accurately and impartially. People will make arguments to persuade you to have a certain belief or behave a certain way. Watch out for persuasive techniques and your propensity to favor something due to your personal bias to assist you in assessing the truth of arguments. Watch out for strong emotions, as these might make it difficult to view an argument.

Draw Inferences: Inferences are assertions founded upon knowledge or belief. Make rational inferences using all the information at your disposal.

Section 2: Skills You Need for Critical Thinking

It's challenging to improve on something you can't identify, even if you desire to become a better critical thinker. Analyzing a scenario or issue and the facts, data, or supporting evidence is known as critical thinking. In its ideal form, critical thinking only considers facts and is conducted objectively, without regard to sentiments, beliefs, or prejudices.

You can only act rationally and intelligently if you can think critically. For instance, a young child who lacks these skills may think tales their parents have told them led the Tooth Fairy to leave money beneath their pillow. However, a critical thinker can soon conclude that the likelihood of such a thing is probably remote—even if they had a few dollars hidden under their pillow.

Best Critical Thinking Techniques

Although there is no unified definition of what constitutes critical thinking, we have narrowed it down to the following ten skills. You can develop your critical thinking skills by concentrating on them.

Identification

Identifying the circumstance or issue and any potential contributing elements is the first stage of the critical thinking process. You can start to explore an issue and its possibilities if you have a clear image of the situation and the people, groups, or causes that may be influenced.

Research

Independent research skills are essential when comparing viewpoints on a subject. The data and figures that support an argument may be out of context or from dubious sources because arguments are supposed to persuade. The best defense against this is independent verification; tracking down the information's source and assessing it.

Identifying Biases

Even the most intelligent people can struggle with this skill since biases can go undetected. Strong critical thinkers try to assess information objectively. Consider yourself a judge who wants to assess the arguments made by each side while also accounting for any biases that the party may have.

Inference

Another crucial talent for mastering critical thinking is the capacity to infer and make inferences from the data provided. There isn't always a summary of the information that explains what it implies. You will frequently have to evaluate the information provided and make judgments based on numerical facts.

When analyzing a scenario, the capacity to infer enables you to extrapolate and identify potential outcomes. It is also crucial to remember that not every inference will be accurate. For instance, you could assume someone is overweight if you read that they weigh 260 pounds. However, other information, such as height and body composition, may cause that conclusion to change.

Determining Relevance

Finding the most crucial information for your attention when faced with a difficult situation is one of the hardest components of thinking critically. In many cases, you'll be presented with information that can appear significant, but it might be just a small piece of knowledge to consider.

Curiosity

Even while it is quite simple to accept everything that is said to you at face value, doing so might lead to disaster when faced with a situation that calls for critical thinking. We are all innately inquisitive, as any parent who has dealt with a barrage of "Why?" queries from a child will attest to. As we age, it's easy to fall into the habit of suppressing our curiosity. However, that is not a successful strategy for critical thinking.

Analysis

The capacity to thoroughly study something, be it an issue, a collection of data, or a text, is a component of critical thinking. Analytical thinkers can evaluate information, decipher its consequences, and effectively communicate those conclusions to others.

Creativity

Creativity and invention are frequent components of critical thinking. You may need to identify patterns in the data you are examining or to develop an original solution. All of this requires a creative vision that can adopt a method that is distinct from all previous methods.

Open-Mindedness

You must set aside any preconceptions or prejudices and study the data you are given to think critically. You must be impartial in your evaluation of ideas.

Problem-Solving

Problem-solving entails understanding a situation, coming up with a solution, putting it into action, and evaluating how well it worked. Nowadays, it is paramount to be someone who can do more than critically analyze material. They must also be able to think of workable solutions.

Section 3: The Barriers to Critical Thinking

Different barriers to critical thinking might interfere with the effectiveness of critical thinking. As an individual, you must become aware of these barriers to combat and remove them.

Barriers to Critical Thinking

Egocentric Mentality

Egocentricity is a natural propensity that is often difficult to resist. Such a barrier forces the individual to focus on oneself and prevents them from empathizing with others or being able to comprehend their concerns. And one of the biggest roadblocks to critical thinking can be one's ego.

This is more of a character problem, and even after numerous tries to change, it might be challenging to do so. Such people make it uncomfortable for others to work with them in a team because they are unable to consider the viewpoint and emotions of others.

Group Thinking

Another dangerous barrier to critical thinking is group thinking, which is likewise very unhealthy. In such a condition, the individual lacks independent judgment in any event. To overcome this, each group member must take a stand, reflect, and articulate their views, beliefs, and opinions. This obstacle exemplifies the adage "too many cooks spoil the broth," as there is no individual activity taken by the person.

Drone Mentality

The drone mentality barrier is characterized by a failure to concentrate during crucial meetings and talks at work. Daily, monotonous tasks frequently cause people to develop a drone mentality.

Conditioning to Socialization

Many of us tend to think within our comfort zones, and we often abstain from thinking outside of those boundaries because of social pressure. Social conditioning creates barriers to critical thinking by causing us to stereotype the objects and people around us and make unwarranted assumptions. To get over this tendency and barrier, cultural and social awareness is necessary.

Biased Experiences and Nature

One of the largest obstacles to critical thinking is having personal biases because they prevent someone from making fair, unbiased, and transparent conclusions. Additionally, it hinders the person's ability to make sound decisions by using logic, experience, and common sense.

Stress

At work and in other situations, we may have too many deadlines to meet, which impacts our ability to use critical thinking. However, working under pressure and against tight deadlines allows some people to hone their critical thinking skills. We frequently choose the option of doing the work without strategic consideration or long-term vision when time is limited, and a deadline must be fulfilled. This is where the obstacle to critical thinking appears.

Arrogance

Arrogance is a negative attitude that frequently impairs one's capacity for critical thought. It creates a person with a closed perspective and the conviction that they already know everything and do not require further education. Arrogance causes a person to fail over the long term because it closes off their learning opportunities and prevents them from understanding the rewards and advantages of critical thinking.

Fierce Nature

Being stubborn is one of the barriers to critical thinking since someone with that personality has their own set of ideologies and beliefs. Individuals who strive for excellent critical thinking must be open to change and let go of their current beliefs to see that the world is highly fluid and fast-paced and necessitates flexibility and adaptability.

Fear

Fear frequently serves as a roadblock, not only to critical thinking but also to growth and development. Their lack of confidence, motivation, and agility makes them less able to think creatively and produce ideas and tactics. Fear can arise from many causes, including anxiety, despair, low self-esteem, and other similar personal factors that impact other areas of life.

Being Lazy

A person who wants to excel in critical thinking must conduct extensive research, read material, and be open to learning new things. If not ready to do so, that becomes a barrier.

Section 4: Asking The Right Questions as a Critical Thinker

Asking the right questions can make the difference between successful and unsuccessful critical thinking. Choosing the right questions can be incredibly effective in the critical thinking process.

1. Make free-form inquiries.

As a critical thinker, you cannot accept the least amount of information from whoever or whatever you are questioning. Yes or No answers can seriously slow down the process of receiving the information and answers you need. Asking questions that will not only lead to the information you need but also reveal more than what you were seeking is key. Here are two examples of what open-ended inquiries look like:

- Instead of asking, *"is this the goal of the scenario?"* ask, *"what is the point of this scenario?"*
- Instead of asking, *"is this your favorite aspect of this scenario?"* ask, *"what do you like best about this situation?"*

2. Steer clear of direct inquiries.

You must escape from your bias and view things from a different perspective to be a critical thinker. Thus, it is crucial to avoid guiding the inquiry in the direction you want it to go. Avoid using judgmental language in your queries and keep them as impartial as possible. For instance:

- Ask, *"what do you think is the best diet that is available?"* instead of, *"do you not believe that a vegan diet is the healthiest diet?"*
- Ask, *"what is the country's current state like?"* instead of *"how awful is the country's situation right now?"*

3. Identify the parameters of your inquiries.

Both guiding a question and leaving it too open might work against the attainment of your goals. That is why, in some cases, you might need to apply your critical thinking with purpose and direction. Make sure you establish a precise structure within which your queries can be addressed. In this way, the answers can become efficient and fast. Try posing inquiries like these:

- Ask, *"which American male tennis player is your favorite?"* instead of, *"who is your favorite tennis player?"*
- Ask, *"where would you choose to reside if you could live anyplace in Southeast Asia?"* instead of, *"where would you live, if you could live anywhere?"*

4. Continue asking questions until you get to what you need.

When you ask only superficial inquiries, it is simple for the information sources you are examining to deceive you and withhold the knowledge you need. Instead of planning your inquiries in advance, be sure to go deeper in the direction of the information you want to follow. Once you have your response, go back to asking more general questions once again to obtain a greater understanding of the entire situation.

5. Every response to your query needs to be supported by credible facts and sources.

Make sure you avoid believing hearsay. Before you accept the information offered to you, find the studies, the science, and several testimonials. To determine whether the material is accurate, look at numerous unrelated and diverse sources. Consider the opposing viewpoint and the facts that support their assertions.

Examples of Critical Question Types

1. Open-ended inquiries: Inspiring in-depth responses.

Why did Rose in Titanic choose to reject a life of privilege? What do you think about the current environmental situation, and how would you try to fix it? What about your work most inspires you, and what about that inspires you so much?

2. Questions with outcomes that show character attributes.

What would you tell a 5-year-old about coding? What two exercises would you pick if you could only do two to stay in shape, and why? Tell me about a time when you had to make a choice based on unreliable data. How did you act?

3. Speculative queries: Made-up examples.

How would you react if you learned that a buddy was having an affair with the spouse of another friend? How would you respond if two employees under your supervision started yelling at each other in the office? What consequences might there be?"

4. Reflective inquiries.

What personal benefits have you derived from this experience? Do you believe there was a more efficient approach to do what you did, and, if so, how would you apply it going forward? How has this procedure facilitated your ability to do related tasks in the future?

Critical Listening

Critical listening is not as popular as active or empathetic listening. Active and empathetic listening have positive connotations, but when we think about the word *critical*, that may not be true. You can find definitions like "offering harsh or disapproving comments or judgments" when you search the term *critical*. This definition is what fuels an inaccurate notion. However, if you search for *critique*, it is defined as "a detailed examination and assessment." If you prefer to think about the grammar of the English language, you may think of critical listening as a verb that means "to evaluate and assess," which has a more accurate meaning.

Critical listening is applying methodical, thorough thought and reasoning to determine if a message makes sense in light of objective facts. Although you can develop it with experience, critical listening is not always easy. Some people never acquire this talent; instead, they believe whatever they hear, even when it conflicts with what they already know. When someone receives information who cannot determine if it is true or accurate, problems might arise. There are five critical listening skills that you need to use when conducting a thorough analysis and assessment:

1) Determining the logic's persuasiveness.
2) Examining potential biases and assumptions.
3) Considering the data.
4) Examining "fit to goals."
5) Evaluating its completeness.

Complex messages might make it more challenging to listen critically. Some presenters may intentionally make their statements difficult to understand to avoid scrutinization. For instance, an administrator presenting a budget can use complicated language and technical jargon to make it challenging for listeners to comprehend the proposed budget and offer insightful inquiries.

There are other approaches to listening for which we will not go into detail: Open listening, necessary for brainstorming or idea development (to generate more ideas), and empathetic listening, used when coaching a team member (to formulate coaching questions). It is important to remember to adopt the most suited listening approach for the current situation.

Section 5: Paul-Elder Critical Thinking Framework

Paul and Elder (1997) assert that decision-makers must grasp two key aspects of thinking to understand how to improve their thinking. They must be able to recognize the different "parts" of their thinking and evaluate how well they employ each one.

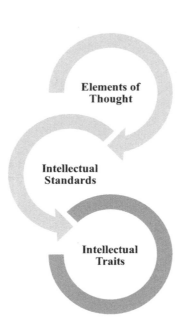

Elements of Thought (Reasoning)

The following are the parts or components of thinking:

- Every argument has a **purpose**.
- Every argument attempts to establish some truth, answer some **question**, or address some issue.
- Every argument makes an **assumption**.
- Every argument takes a **point of view.**
- Facts, **information,** and proof support inferences.
- Language, culture, concepts, and ideas all serve to express and form reasoning.
- All forms of thinking include **inferences** or interpretations that allow us to reach conclusions and provide context to facts.
- Every argument has a point, or it has **implications** and results.

Intellectual Standards

The level of reasoning is determined using the intellectual standards that apply to these components. Knowing these requirements demands the ability to think critically. According to Paul and Elder (1997, 2006), the ultimate objective is for the norms of reasoning to be ingrained in all thinking so they may serve as the road map for ever-improving logic. The criteria for intellect include the terms listed below.

Clarity

- Can you give more details?
- Could you provide an example of what you mean?

Accuracy

- How might we verify that?
- How might we determine if that is the case?
- How might we confirm or examine that?

Precision

- Could you be more detailed?
- Could you please elaborate?
- Can you be more specific?

Relevance

- What connection does that have to the issue?
- What relevance does that have to the query?
- How does that aid in solving the problem?

Depth

- What are the challenges in this?
- What are some of the nuances in this issue?
- What are some of the challenges we must overcome?

Breadth

- Do we need to consider this from a different angle?
- Do we need to take a different viewpoint into account?
- Do we need to consider things from other angles?

Logic

- Does this make sense taken as a whole?
- Do your opening and closing paragraphs make sense together?
- Does the evidence support what you're saying?

Significance

- Is this the most crucial issue to consider?
- Is this the main concept to concentrate on?
- Which of these details is the most crucial?

Fairness

- Is my reasoning reasonable in this situation?
- Am I considering how others might think?
- Is my goal reasonable given the circumstances?
- Do I use my ideas in a way that is consistent with knowledgeable usage, or do I twist them to suit my needs?

Intellectual Traits

When the standards of thinking are consistently applied to the components of thinking, the following intellectual qualities are developed: Humility, bravery, empathy, independence, integrity, persistence, faith in reason, and fairness.

Qualities of an Experienced Critical Thinker

Regular application of the intellectual qualities results in a well-developed critical thinker who can:

- Pose important queries and issues and formulate them clearly and exactly;
- Collect and evaluate pertinent data, then use abstract concepts to understand them well;
- Arrive at well-thought-out conclusions and solutions and evaluate them considering pertinent standards and criteria;
- Consider various ways of thinking with an open mind, recognizing and evaluating them as necessary based on their premises, implications, and application; and
- Effectively communicate with others to come up with solutions to challenging issues.

Paul-Elder Critical Thinking Framework in Everyday Life

Real news vs. Fake news

Think about your media savvy for a second. Can you distinguish between a reliable news source and a creative advertisement? According to a recent Stanford University research, 82% of the kids polled couldn't tell the difference between a sponsored piece and a news item. Schools may contribute to the issue by reducing the formal education of critical thinking skills and assuming that today's "digital native" teenagers can distinguish between the two without practice or instruction. You excel in a variety of areas. However, you have honed the skills you are proficient in. How can you then practice differentiating fact from fiction? Talking with your family and friends about media sources is one approach to do this. Learn how and why people choose the sources of information they do. Ask each other inquiries regularly for analyzing sources.

Do your friends have all the knowledge?

It's alluring to think that your pals are the beginning and end of the world. Friends are undoubtedly valuable. It is beneficial to consider how a group affects our life, though. Take a hard look at your pals to learn how to apply critical thinking in daily life. Are there any forbidden topics in your social circle? Are you required to behave or appear in a certain way?

Sometimes when a group member decides something is cool, everyone tries to live up to that standard, no matter what each individual thinks. The issue is that there are numerous ways to define almost every circumstance. What one person considers stupid may be cool to another. Improve your capacity to reframe how you perceive the world based on your terms. Find a time when your friends only see the bad in things. Is there an alternative, more optimistic perspective? You may not be ready to express an opposing viewpoint yet. That's okay, too. Just learn to consider multiple angles.

Section 6: Fallacies

Common misconceptions known as fallacies will impeach the logic of your argument. Fallacious arguments might be unfounded or irrelevant, and they are simple to spot since they come with no supporting data. Avoid common fallacies in your assertions and watch out for them in others'.

Several Common Examples of Everyday Fallacies

The Fallacy of the False Start

This fallacy occurs when your opponent misrepresents or oversimplifies your argument (by constructing a "straw man") to make it easier to attack or refute. Speakers who employ this fallacy present a superficially similar but ultimately unjustified version of your actual position to create the impression that they can easily defeat you rather than thoroughly address it.

Example

John: We ought to pay someone to overhaul our website, in my opinion.

Lola: You're suggesting that we spend our money on outside vendors rather than expanding our design team? In the long term, that will be detrimental to our business.

The Bandwagon Fallacy

A statement is not always true simply because many people believe it to be so. Though it is frequently used as a stand-alone defense of the validity of an argument, popularity alone is insufficient. This type of argument does not consider whether the population validating the argument is truly qualified to do so or whether there is opposing evidence.

Example

Billboards are objectively the best type of advertising because most people think that businesses should spend more money on them.

The Fallacy of Relying on Authority

While not always incorrect, appeals to authority can quickly become dangerous when too much trust is placed in one person's judgment, especially when that person is attempting to justify something outside of their area of expertise.

Example

We should continue utilizing the same method even if our Q4 figures were significantly lower than usual because our CEO, Barbara, feels this is the best course of action.

A False Dilemma Fallacy

This widespread misconception misleads by splitting complicated issues into two sides that are essentially at odds with one another. The false dilemma fallacy holds that there are only two conceivable outcomes that are mutually incompatible rather than realizing that most (if not all) issues may be thought upon from a range of viewpoints.

Example

We have two options: Either we embrace Barbara's suggestion or we just let the project fail. Nothing further needs to be done.

The Fallacy of Quick Generalization

This error occurs when broad assumptions are made based on shaky or insufficient data. In other words, they dismiss plausible counterarguments and make assumptions about the truth of a claim that has some but insufficient evidence to support it.

Example

Two members of my team who took public speaking training have developed into more motivated workers. This demonstrates why, to increase employee engagement, public speaking lessons should be made mandatory for the entire organization.

The Slothful Induction Fallacy

The opposite of the previously mentioned fallacy of quick generalization is slothful induction. This fallacy happens when there is enough logical evidence to conclude that something is true, but the person contests the conclusion, attributing the result to chance or something unrelated.

Example

Even if every project Brad has managed in the last two years has run way behind schedule, I still think we can blame this on uncontrollable events rather than his project management skills.

The Correlation and Causation Fallacy

If two things appear to be related, it does not necessarily follow that one of them caused the other (we will discuss this more in detail later). Even though it may appear to be a simple fallacy to identify, it can be difficult to do so in practice, especially if you truly want to discover causation between two pieces of information to support your claim.

Example

Our blog's readership decreased in April. In April, we also altered the color of the header of our blog. This indicates that a change in the blog header's color resulted in fewer views in April.

The Anecdotal Evidence Fallacy

This fallacy uses examples from personal experience in place of rational backing. Arguments that mainly depend on anecdotal evidence could overlook the fact that a single (potentially isolated) case cannot provide proof for a larger assertion.

Example

After making the whole text on their landing page bright red, one of our clients witnessed a twofold boost in conversions. Thus, a tried-and-true method for boosting conversions is to make all text red.

The Middle Ground Fallacy

This fallacy assumes that a compromise between two radically opposing viewpoints is always true. In this type of argument, a compromise between the two extremes is fallacious because it ignores the possibility that one or both could be completely correct or incorrect.

Example

Lisa must be a successful entrepreneur because she sold her first startup to a powerful tech corporation. (She disregards the fact that since then, four of her ventures have failed.)

The Fallacy of Personal Skepticism

It does not necessarily follow that something is false if it is difficult to understand how or why it is true. A claim cannot be declared invalid because of a single instance or widespread ignorance.

Example

John believes that changing the company website will not bring any value because it is hard to understand how and why this will bring any value.

Section 7: Cognitive Biases

Cognitive Bias: What Is It?

When people absorb and interpret information from their environment, they can make systematic cognition errors that impact their decisions and judgments. This phenomenon is known as cognitive bias. Although powerful, the human brain has its limits. Your brain tries to make information processing as simple as possible, which often creates cognitive biases. Biases frequently serve as generalizations that facilitate quick decision-making and aid in making sense of the world. Some of these biases include memories. Your memory of an experience may be affected for many reasons, leading to biased thinking and decision-making.

Other cognitive biases could influence attentional issues. People must choose what they pay attention to in the world around them since attention is not an infinite resource. Because of this, unnoticeable biases may infiltrate your thinking and affect how you perceive the world. Amos Tversky and Daniel Kahneman, two psychologists, initially introduced the idea of cognitive bias in 1972. Since then, researchers have identified numerous biases that influence judgment in many contexts, such as social behavior, cognition, behavioral economics, education, management, healthcare, business, and finance.

Logic Fallacy vs. Cognitive Bias

Logic fallacies and cognitive biases are two different concepts that are occasionally confused. A logical fallacy results from a flaw in an argument's logic, and cognitive biases are the result of thought-processing errors attributed to memory, attention, attribution, and so on.

Types

Actor-observer bias is the propensity to blame external factors for your actions while blaming internal factors for the acts of others. For instance, you might think that the high cholesterol levels of others are caused by poor nutrition and inactivity, while you ascribe your own to genetics.

Anchoring bias is the propensity to place excessive weight on the first piece of knowledge you find. For instance, if you discover the typical cost of a car is a certain amount, you might stop looking for better offers because you will consider any sum below that a fantastic deal. By presenting the initial information for consideration, you can leverage this bias to influence the expectations of others.

Attentional bias is the tendency to focus on some things while neglecting others. For instance, while choosing a car, you might focus on how the outside and inside look and feel but disregard the vehicle's safety record and fuel efficiency.

Availability heuristic is when you give more weight to information that comes to mind quickly. If something is more present in your mind, you tend to overestimate the possibility and likelihood of similar situations happening in the future.

Confirmation bias is the tendency to favor information that supports your current opinions while rejecting data that contradicts them.

False consensus effect is the propensity to exaggerate how much other people concur with you is known as the false consensus effect.

Functional fixedness is the propensity to view things as only functioning in a specific manner. For instance, you might not think to use a large wrench to push a nail into the wall if you don't have a hammer. If you don't have a corkboard to pin things to, you could assume you don't need thumbtacks and fail to explore their various uses. This effect might also apply to how people perform their jobs, such as failing to see that a personal assistant has the aptitude to take on a leadership position.

Halo effect is when your perception of someone affects how you view and consider their character. This effect is particularly true when a person's physical appeal affects how you perceive other traits.

Optimism bias makes you think that you are more likely to succeed and less likely to experience bad luck than your peers.

Self-serving bias is the propensity to blame unsatisfactory outcomes on outside factors and to take credit for positive ones. For instance, when you win a poker hand, it's because of your ability to gauge the other players' intentions and understand the odds. When you lose, however, it's because the dealer dealt you a bad hand.

Dunning-Kruger effect is when someone believes they are more intelligent and capable than they are.

Impact of Cognitive Bias

Cognitive biases may lead to distorted thinking. For instance, several biases frequently affect people's beliefs about conspiracies. However, not all cognitive biases are harmful. Many of these biases, according to psychologists, have an adaptive function in that they facilitate speedy decision-making. If we are in a dangerous or threatening scenario, this is essential. For instance, if you are walking down a dark alley and a dark figure appears to be following you, cognitive bias may cause you to believe that the shadow is a thief and that you should leave the area immediately. When you must make quick judgments, mental shortcuts can frequently help you avoid danger, even if the shadow may have only been a flag fluttering in the air.

How Cognitive Bias Impacts our Everyday Life: Examples

Gender prejudice in the workplace is one element of cognitive bias that has been thoroughly researched and documented. Women typically do not hold senior positions. For instance, just 15.2% of the top positions in the US Fortune 500 businesses in 2010 were held by women (Soares, 2010), though the situation has improved recently. Women's salaries are also frequently lower than those of their male counterparts.

Anyone who uses self-reported data should be concerned about the social desirability bias. Businesses that conduct internal surveys on subjects that can negatively reflect an employee need to be aware of how the social desirability bias will impair the reliability of their results. Surveyors should try to reframe their questions to be less direct, employ formal tests, or anonymize responses since they are aware that people change their answers to look more socially desirable.

Personal finance is another area of our lives where prejudices can have disastrous results. At least 40 cognitive biases, as suggested by Jacobs-Lawson, Hershey, and Austin (2012), hurt our capacity to make wise financial decisions and prevent us from effectively planning for retirement. These biases include the following:

• Halo effect: Just because the real estate agent was kind, it doesn't necessarily guarantee the deal is good.
• Optimistic overconfidence: "I'll be all right in the future, so I don't need to save that much now."

Section 8: Key Habits to Adopt to Improve Your Critical Thinking

Understanding Assumptions

Separating fact from opinion is paramount in the critical thinking process. Leveraging specific, reliable evidence to support true claims or that can be rationally inferred to be true is very important.

Example:

The supposition that follows is an opinion: Our best clients will cease purchasing our product if we increase the price.

The following presumption instead is backed up by data: If we increase our pricing by $5, a market analysis done earlier this year predicts a 10% decline in sales to our Tier 1 customers.

Considering Arguments

Ask questions to ascertain whether a person is relying on evidence to back their claims. To find out if a perspective is supported by facts, evidence, or experience, pose open-ended questions. Think about how logical, trustworthy, and applicable this knowledge is to your circumstance. Strongly worded assertions made authoritatively may be mistaken for fact rather than opinion.

Ask:

- On what do you base your opinion?
- What supporting data do you have?
- What makes you think that the data is reliable?
- What makes you believe that this would apply to this issue?

Identify the Situation

Consider the information carefully before choosing a plan of action.

Ask:

- How critical is this circumstance?
- What time frame do I have to find a solution?
- Who is impacted by this circumstance, and what are their goals or concerns?
- What tools do I have at my disposal?

Making Judgments

The finest findings are logically supported by adequate, reliable data.

Ask:

- What suppositions do I (and others) hold?
- How much of these suppositions can I believe?
- What justifications are they offering for me to accept? How convincing are these claims?
- What inferences may I make based on the facts I've reviewed?
- What should we do in the best possible way?

A Practical Example

Consider an illustration of a hand holding a smartphone with the text "Study: Cats are better than dogs" shown on it. Let's examine how you can use critical thinking to assess online content. Let's say one of your friends shares a news story on social media, and you are intrigued by the headline. Using your automatic thought process, you might accept it as a true statement and carry on. But if you were using critical thought, you would first evaluate the material at hand and pose some queries:

- What is the source?
- Is the headline possibly deceptive?
- What are the prevailing beliefs of my friend?

Now, consider a screenshot of a smartphone article with the phrases "Super Cat Blog" and "According to the poll of cat owners" underlined.

You can determine whether you believe the article to be reliable after considering all the data you found. Many practical situations call for the use of critical thinking. It can aid in better decision-making, increase your employability, and help your overall understanding of the world.

Section 9: Deductive vs. Inductive Reasoning

There are two distinct methods of conducting research: inductive reasoning and deductive reasoning. The former strategy concentrates on creating a theory, whereas the latter evaluates an existing theory.

Definition of Inductive Reasoning

Inductive reasoning is a method of logical thought in which a conclusion is reached by combining observations that are thought to be true to develop more comprehensive generalizations and hypotheses.

Definition of Deductive Reasoning

In contrast, deductive reasoning operates in the opposite direction from inductive reasoning. It is a logical thought process that moves from the more general to the more specific. To reach a logical conclusion, it makes use of logical premises and basic assumptions.

Deductive vs. Inductive Reasoning

- Inductive reasoning works by going from a single observation to a more broad-based, generalized conclusion.
- Deductive reasoning starts with a general assertion and uses a logical conclusion to support it.
- Inductive reasoning is frequently referred to as a "bottom-up technique" because it begins with an observation, is used to identify patterns, generate hypotheses, and then lead to conclusions or theories.
- Because you start with a theory, develop it into a hypothesis, test the hypothesis, and then arrive at a logical affirmation, deductive reasoning is frequently referred to as a "top-down approach."
- The truth of the premises does not automatically imply the truth of the conclusion in inductive reasoning.
- If the premises are true, then the conclusion must also be true in deductive reasoning.

Examples of Inductive and Deductive Reasoning

Inductive Reasoning Example

Observation: The dogs who live in my area get along well.

Recognize a pattern: All dogs are amicable.

Theorem: Every dog is amiable.

Deductive Reasoning Example

Theorem: Every dog is amiable.

Hypothesis: Theoretically, every pet dog in my area is amiable.

Test Hypothesis: Watch all the dogs in the area as a test.

Conclusion: The hypothesis is false because 7 out of the neighborhood's 23 dogs were aggressive.

Inductive Reasoning Usage

Every day, we apply inductive reasoning to situations like estimating your departure time from home for work based on traffic or deciding on a unique employee wellness program in light of employee input.

Deductive Reasoning Usage

Deductive reasoning is frequently applied to problem-solving and decision-making. You can use deductive reasoning to get to the root of the customer's issue and use that information to provide the ideal solution or to create a new store design that will draw in more consumers and boost revenue.

Approach to Research Using Inductive Reasoning

A conclusion is reached through inductive reasoning, a logical thought process that combines observations with experiential data. Every time you examine a collection of data and draw general inferences based on knowledge from previous experiences, you are using inductive reasoning. Inductive research is frequently employed when there is little published material on a subject. This is because the concept cannot be tested using any existing theories. The three stages of the inductive approach are as follows:

1) Observe
2) Recognize a pattern
3) Construct a theory

Let's look at the example below to better grasp this strategy:

Observation	Recognize a Pattern	Construct a Theory
Both free editing apps, App A and B, have technical issues.	All free editing apps that have been seen have app bugs.	App bugs are present in all free editing programs.

Research Methodologies Using Deductive Reasoning

When applying deductive reasoning in research, you begin with a theory. Then, based on this theory, more specific, testable hypotheses are generated. These are then further distilled into observations that let us test the hypothesis to see if the information supports or rejects it. Therefore, the deductive training method can be divided into the following four stages:

1) Start with an established theory.
2) Create a hypothesis based on the theory that already exists.
3) Gather information to test the hypothesis.
4) Review the findings to determine whether the data confirms or refutes the hypothesis.

Let's look at the example below to better grasp this strategy:

Start With an Established Theory	Create a Hypothesis	Test the Hypothesis	Review the Findings/Results
App bugs are present in all inexpensive editing programs.	Users will encounter app bugs if they choose an inexpensive editing app.	Gather information on affordable editing apps.	The majority of the inexpensive editing apps—20 out of 50—don't have any bugs. = Disprove the Theory

Examples of Inductive Reasoning

Here a few different examples of inductive logic to obtain a better understanding of it. Try to identify how it is used.

- At seven in the morning, Jennifer always leaves for school. Jennifer is constantly punctual. Jennifer, therefore, believes that if she leaves for school at 7:00 a.m. today, she will arrive on time.
- In this region, the North is the source of every windstorm. In the distance, I can make out a sizable dust cloud. That direction, therefore, must be North.
- The living room chair is red. The dining room chair is red. The bedroom chair is red. The home's chairs are all red.
- Michael recently relocated from Chicago. Michael is a redhead. Consequently, everyone from Chicago has red hair.
- We have only ever seen brown chickens. In this location, all chickens must be brown.
- John has a great swimming stroke. His household owns a pool. Mary, John's sister, must be a skilled swimmer as well.
- Today's park has only little brown dogs. All little dogs must therefore be brown.
- Every child in this childcare facility enjoys playing with Legos. All kids must enjoy playing with Legos.
- Almost every home on South Street is in disrepair. South Street is the home of Sherry. Her home is probably in danger of collapse.
- We regularly have thunderstorms in May. We're going to receive a thunderstorm because it's May.

Examples of Deductive Reasoning

Deductive reasoning skills are regularly put to the test in daily life. Have you ever questioned when you would use the skills you learned in algebra class? Those lessons, at the very least, were designed to challenge our capacity for deduction. Keep in mind that if a = b and b = c, then a = c. Let's explain that with some more examples:

- Every number with a 0 or a 5 is divisible by 5. 35 has a 5 at the end, so it must be divisible by 5.
- All bird species have feathers. Every robin is a bird. Because of this, robins have feathers.
- Driving on snowy roads is hazardous. It would be risky to drive on the streets because they are currently frozen.
- Cats have an excellent sense of smell. Fluffy has a good sense of smell because she is a cat.
- All plants engage in photosynthesis. Cacti, as plants, engage in photosynthesis.
- Beef is red meat. All meat contains iron. Consequently, beef contains iron.
- Less than 90 degrees is an acute angle. Given that it is 40 degrees, this angle must be acute.
- Noble gases all have stability. Helium is stable since it is a noble gas.
- Elephants' bodies are made up of cells, and every cell has DNA. Elephants have DNA.
- Every horse has a mane. Because the Arabian is a horse, they have manes.

Section 10: The Importance of Patterns

Although the human brain is an ideal machine for pattern detection, we rarely use it. Patterns are everywhere, and the ability to see patterns is unquestionably essential for success in any endeavor. They are present in mathematics, nature, the arts, music, literature, business, and so on. In situations that could otherwise seem chaotic, patterns help create a feeling of order. Researchers have discovered that comprehending and seeing recurrent patterns enables us to form educated predictions, assumptions, and hypotheses; it also aids the development of critical thinking and logical abilities that are crucial for success. The study of patterns may be used across all subject areas and allows a wide range of opportunities for application. They are necessary for creative thinking and are enablers of critical thinking and problem-solving. Patterns can help us by:

- **Avoiding creating new problems.** Knowing the patterns in your area of concern saves you time and allows you to speed up understanding.
- **Serving as a conduit for creativity.** A pattern can be used a million times and never be used the same way twice. Knowing a pattern allows you to explore all the possible ways to unfold it. However, by emphasizing a pattern's limitations, challenges, and ramifications, it provides precise but adaptable instructions.
- **Opening up discoveries.** When patterns are combined, new forms emerge.

Patterns have tremendous power if our brains are properly engaged ability to recognize, use, and create them. Their use can mean the difference between long-term success and failure in many situations.

Pattern Recognition

The process of identifying and comprehending patterns is known as pattern recognition. It is a crucial skill because it lets us use prior knowledge and techniques to deal with several issues simultaneously. For example, if we had treated each Coronavirus patient as a different case during the outbreak of the COVID-19 pandemic, we would never have been able to recognize that they were all affected by the same virus. Without looking for patterns in their cases, scientists and doctors would not have been able to comprehend the epidemiology and symptoms of the outbreak. Pattern recognition is not only used in science or math. We use this skill in our daily lives, from the time we are infants to the time we reach adulthood. For example, babies learn emotions by recognizing familiar patterns in **facial features**.

We utilize mnemonics—memory aids—like **songs, slogans,** or **mental images**, to help us remember information. Nearly all mnemonic devices rely on patterns, such as when you recite BODMAS to remember the sequence of mathematical operations or VIBGYOR to recall the color spectrum. The basis of **music** is the playing of sounds and notes in patterns that we refer to as rhythm and melody. If you look at your everyday activities, it may be clear that your behavior has evolved into a **routine**.

It is crucial to find ways to include pattern recognition in our critical thinking and problem-solving techniques from a young age since it can make us more efficient. You can start practicing active pattern recognition with the simplest things and then move gradually to more complex areas. For example, you can search for patterns in the surrounding environment by determining traits and attributes and locating them in various locations. Playing Sudoku a few times per week can also help, as it allows you to hone your computational thinking abilities while emphasizing pattern detection.

Start looking for patterns in your life, and I guarantee it will benefit you greatly.

Patterns Across Different Areas

Patterns in Nature: Natural patterns are observable morphological regularities seen in nature. These recurring patterns may occasionally be described quantitatively and occur in a variety of circumstances. Examples of natural patterns include symmetries, trees, spirals, meanders, waves, foams, tessellations, fissures, and stripes. Among the early Greek philosophers who studied patterns to explain order in nature were Plato, Pythagoras, and Empedocles. The concept of visual patterns as we know it now developed progressively through time.

Patterns in Art: These patterns may be the repetition or echoes of an artwork's parts to convey a feeling of harmony, balance, contrast, rhythm, or movement. Patterns in art are employed for both ornamental and structural purposes. A compositional pattern of lines and forms, for instance, might be used by an artist to arrange the composition of a piece of art. They may work on the composition's visual features to give the piece a more ornamental pattern of color, tone, and texture.

Patterns in Math: Most individuals naturally consider patterns in mathematics. A subtle capacity to identify and explain trends is needed for all kinds of mathematical tasks, including using money and creating budgets.

Patterns in Music: Music is made of recurring patterns, and people who can identify these patterns are usually stronger musicians and composers. This is so that we can reproduce the musical patterns we hear and educate ourselves to play after we have a basic understanding of how music is made.

Patterns in Language: Children learn language primarily through imitation. Children pick up politeness and appropriate behavior in this way. Every language contains recognizable patterns that aid our memory of when and how to express thoughts.

Patterns in Emotion: Children need to understand the kinds of comments that irritate people, the consequences of their actions, and how to shield themselves from negative feelings. They can successfully manage life while teaching themselves once they notice these patterns.

Patterns in Business: Businesses may use recurring solutions to typical problems. Patterns also aid in the preservation of an architectural style throughout the organization.

Pattern Utilization

The importance of recognizing patterns is due to the next step, which is pattern utilization. If we can see patterns, we can use them for our benefit. Let's see some examples of the advantages of using patterns in life. Consider my friend Jane who is a finance professional. Although you might not associate her job with the STEM fields, technology and math keep her day running smoothly. Her responsibilities include data analysis and creating models that predict potential future outcomes. Jane searches for similarities in everything she examines to predict what will happen if her organization makes a specific decision in the future. As she develops her estimates, she considers other businesses that have made comparable decisions, the investments they made or did not make, and the outcomes. Jane focuses on situations where patterns do not behave as she would expect. This allows her company to see the big picture of the likely outcomes of its decisions, including potential negative outcomes and their likelihood of occurring. When I asked Jane how she used patterns in her workday, she replied, "Patterns! Pattern recognition accounts for 75% of my work."

I also inquired another friend, John, who is employed by a pharmaceutical company, "Where do you apply patterns at work?" John is a chemist, so he is unquestionably a member of the STEM field. This sparked a lengthy debate between John and me about the importance of patterns AND structures in science: "I seek patterns in chemical structures and the outcomes they cause in biological tests to make better pharmaceuticals," he said when I asked him about his daily activities. He looks for trends in the data to determine a new, potentially superior technique for changing the molecule structure. John looks and uses patterns to devise strategies for improving the molecular structures of drugs so that they can do what they're supposed to do.

In the social sphere, we see people adopting patterns every day in fashion, technology, behavior, and so on. Businesses also use widespread solutions to recurring business problems. Think about your day. How can you use what you know about spotting patterns to make predictions, make decisions, make changes, or simply be more effective? Introduce the practice of pattern recognition and pattern utilization in your everyday life until it becomes second nature to you!

Section 11: Understanding Causation and Correlation

A correlation indicates a statistical relationship between two variables. Causation happens when a change in one variable results in a change in another variable. You may have heard the adage "correlation doesn't imply causation" while conducting research. Although correlation and causality are linked concepts, knowing how they are different will help you in your ability to evaluate and interpret data critically.

Difference

When one variable changes, the other does too, according to correlation, which describes a link between the variables. A statistical indication of the link between variables is a correlation. They covariate, meaning that they fluctuate simultaneously. But a direct or indirect causal relationship isn't always to blame for this covariation.

The concept of causation instead refers to when there is a cause-and-effect link between the variables. The two variables have a causal relationship as well as a correlation with one another. Although causation always implies correlation, a correlation may not necessarily imply causation.

Why Does Correlation Not Always Imply Causation?

When there is a correlation but not causation it means that there is the so-called **third variable problem**, a confounding variable has an impact on both variables, giving the impression that they are causally related when they are not. For instance, there is a strong correlation between ice cream sales and sunburn rate, although no causal relationship exists between the two. Instead, a third variable—strong, sunny days—affects both variables independently.

When two variables correlate and maybe have a causal link, but it is impossible to determine which variable impacts the other, we refer to the **directionality problem.** For instance, there is a link between low vitamin D levels and depression, although it is unclear whether depression results in lower vitamin D intake or low vitamin D levels induce depression.

Utilize an appropriate research strategy to discern between correlational and causal links. Experimental research methods can test causation, but correlational research designs can only show correlational ties between variables.

Correlational Analysis Examples

Example # 1

You run a survey to test the hypothesis that self-esteem and physical activity levels are related. Participants are questioned about their current exercise habits and their degree of self-worth. You discover that self-esteem and physical activity levels are positively correlated, with lower physical activity levels being linked to lower self-esteem and greater physical activity levels being linked to better self-esteem.

Example # 2

To determine if exposure to violent media is linked to aggressiveness, you gather data on kids' video game usage and behavioral traits. You question parents and instructors about their students' actions in a survey, and you ask them to say how many hours a week their students spend playing violent video games. You find a significant correlation between the two: children who play violent video games for long periods exhibit more aggressive conduct.

The Third Variable Issue, an Example

Parental attention is a confounding factor that may affect how frequently children use violent video games and their behavioral tendencies in your study on violent video games and aggression. Children who receive poor parental care are more likely to play violent video games and engage in aggressive conduct. However, if paternal attention is not included in the analysis, you can only infer a correlation between aggressiveness and violent video game playing time. All you can say when two variables are correlated is that changes in one variable happen simultaneously with changes in the other but not the one affects the other.

Difficulty With Direction

Understanding what variable caused the change of the other one or vice versa can be hard. You must present a directional link with no other possible explanations to prove causality. One variable may affect the other in a unidirectional relationship, or both variables may have an impact on a bidirectional interaction. An experimental design may test each potential path individually, however, a correlational design won't be able to differentiate between any of these options. If we take the example from earlier, there could be three possible causal connections between the variables of physical exercise and self-esteem:

1) Exercise may have an impact on self-esteem.
2) Self-esteem may have an impact on exercise.
3) Exercise and self-esteem may both have an impact on one another.

In correlational research, there is little research control, and the directionality of a link is unknown. You run the danger of determining the relationship in the wrong direction or reverse causality.

Causal Analysis

Controlled experiments are the only way to show that two variables are causally related. To establish causation, experiments evaluate formal predictions, known as hypotheses. Since experiments have a high level of internal validity, you can prove cause-and-effect connections with some degree of certainty. Because an independent variable is changed before a dependent variable's change is measured, directionality can be established. As an illustration, check the directionality of your experimental plan.

You experiment to test if self-esteem is influenced by physical exercise. You implement a physical activity intervention and track self-esteem changes. Your physical exercise intervention must occur before any apparent change in self-esteem to create directionality. You must also plan for a new experiment to determine whether self-esteem can affect physical activity levels to determine whether this link is reciprocal. By employing casual assignment and control groups, you can also get rid of the impact of third variables in a controlled experiment.

Random assignment is used for the participant characteristics of the groups to be equivalent and similar. Each participant is randomly assigned to either a control or an experimental group. The influences of the third variable participant characteristics, for example, age or mental health level, that could affect your results, should be eliminated by random assignment.

The experimental group receives the physical activity intervention, whereas the control group receives a comparable but unrelated intervention. Any differences between groups can be attributed to your intervention by holding all other factors constant (apart from the treatment for your independent variable).

Section 12: The 8 Habits of Effective Critical Thinkers

Critical thinking abilities take time to develop. Keeping an eye on these eight habits will help you become more adept at critical thinking. By developing better critical thinking you will be able to better face the challenges of a constantly changing world and improve your daily decision-making.

Habit #1: They are more concerned with doing things correctly than with being correct.

They can set aside their egos and admit they don't have to know all the answers. They aren't afraid to own their ignorance or errors. They understand the value of seeking out the best information available and raising inquiries.

Habit #2: They refrain from assuming the worst and making snap decisions.

Before acting, they take the time to learn as much as they can to better grasp a complicated situation. They understand that some choices have more significant outcomes than others and that these choices demand closer examination.

Habit #3: They don't take information at face value.

To learn more about what lies behind the data, they enquire. They are aware that it is crucial to verify the accuracy of the facts as well as to be aware of the possibility of material being presented in a way that serves a specific purpose. They also know how to ask about material that might have been overlooked since it does not support a particular viewpoint.

Habit #4: They refrain from overanalyzing, which results in indecision.

While avoiding the pitfall of shaping the data to meet a specific goal, they seek clarity by looking for order or patterns in the data. They can determine when they have enough information to make a judgment by considering both the forest (the overall picture) and the trees (the specifics). They are aware that they will never have all the knowledge they would like, but they are sure that once they have thoroughly and objectively examined the material at hand, they will probably come to wise judgments.

Habit #5: They continually learn and strive to be educated.

They often read and educate themselves to learn about a variety of topics and concerns. This information they obtain could be crucial for making decisions now and in the future.

Habit #6: They exhibit adaptability by being open to hearing different viewpoints.

They strive to comprehend other points of view. They can position their approach more effectively and demonstrate their faith in their capacity for reasoning by being able to see multiple perspectives on a given subject.

Habit #7: They critically evaluate themselves.

They can explain how they concluded so that others can grasp their thought process and reasoning. They examine themselves and are sensitive to their prejudices, asking themselves things like, "Do I have all the essential information? What are the potential ramifications if my conclusions are accurate?" When given more information that allows for better understanding, individuals are willing to revise their opinions.

Habit #8: They have a unique behavioral pattern.

They are self-assured but not arrogant, thoughtful but action-oriented, and decisive while displaying sound reasoning. When the stakes are high and the situation is grey, they can exhibit patience. Compared to the average individual, they read more, and they express themselves clearly. They are capable of autonomous thought but value various viewpoints. When anything goes wrong, they take responsibility for it and try to figure out what went wrong so they may learn from it.

Section 13: Key Critical Thinking Steps

Developing the Correct Skills and Mindset

Every day, we make a lot of decisions, and whether we know it or not, we are all critical thinkers. Every time we consider our options, organize our tasks, or consider the consequences of our choices, we are engaging in critical thinking. It's an essential ability that enables us to weed out false information and make informed choices. In this section, we will discuss the key skills to develop to strengthen our critical thinking abilities and establish a critical thinking attitude.

Principles of Critical Thinking

Critical thinkers have several essential traits that enable them to challenge both the validity of the information and their assumptions. To improve your critical thinking abilities, concentrate on the following areas:

- **Curiosity.** It's essential to have the ability and willingness to consider unconventional strategies and innovative concepts, consider "what if" scenarios, and test your theories. Remain receptive to fresh information. Look for facts that contradict your claims or opposing viewpoints, and when anything is unclear, ask for clarification. You can then reevaluate your thoughts and come to well-informed conclusions.
- **Logical Thought.** It's crucial to prioritize reasoning over feeling. Control your emotions and be cautious in your judgments because while emotion can be inspiring, it can also cause you to act hastily and foolishly. Recognize when a conclusion is false and when it is based on fact.
- **Self-Awareness.** Our values and beliefs indirectly influence many of the choices we make in life. Because they are frequently unconscious, it can be challenging to recognize them in ourselves. You can think

consciously about the opinions you hold and the decisions you make by developing self-awareness. By doing so, you'll put yourself in a position to make more informed decisions.

Steps for Better Critical Thinking

Step 1—Gather Information

Gather information, facts, and opinions on the problem you need to address. Draw from your prior knowledge and consult fresh sources of information to further your understanding. Think about your knowledge gaps and try to fill them. Additionally, search for data that contradicts your presumptions and ideas. Make sure to confirm the credibility and legitimacy of your sources. Not all of what you read is accurate! Make sure your information is accurate by asking the following questions:

- Are the sources of your information reliable? (Reputable authors, dependable coworkers or peers, well-known trade journals, websites, blogs, etc.)
- Is the data you've gathered up to date?
- Has the information been openly criticized?
- Are there any mistakes or flaws in the information?
- Is there any proof to back up or validate the data you have gathered?
- Is there any subjectivity or prejudice in the data you have gathered? (For instance, is it supported by evidence rather than opinion?)

Step 2—Analysis

Now consider and understand the data you have gathered. What are the most important conclusions and takeaways? What is suggested by the evidence? Based on what you have discovered, begin to construct one or two potential arguments. You'll need to sift through the volume of data for the specifics, so exercise your talents of observation to spot any trends or resemblances. After that, you can expand and examine these trends to generate sane projections for the future.

Step 3—Evaluation

Use the laws of reason (induction, deduction, and analogy) to evaluate an argument's validity. You must be able to evaluate an argument's importance and veracity to place it in the proper context. You can only make a wise conclusion after giving all the arguments and possibilities careful thought.

Step 4—Continuous Improvement

You can take some time to consider what you've learned and what you found difficult. Take a step back from the specifics of your choice or issue and consider the whole situation. Write down the knowledge you gained from your experiences and observations so that you can leverage the learning for the next occasion.

Section 14: Exercises to Develop Critical Thinking

As a critical thinker, the top critical thinking abilities that you should hone and concentrate on are as follows:

- The capacity to connect thoughts. This includes finding out how things are related and which ones are unnecessary.
- The capacity to organize arguments. This involves the components of constructing a pertinent, convincing, and useful argument.
- The capacity to spot contradictions. Finding flaws in defense is how to get at the truth.

Daily Critical Thinking Practice Exercises

The process of learning never ends. You are exposed to fresh experiences every day, giving you the chance to learn new things. You don't need to experience stress or pressure, though, during the process. There are enjoyable and simple exercises you can do to develop your creative thinking. The critical thinking exercises listed below can help you hone and build your fundamental critical thinking abilities:

1. A reading practice. Reading is a fantastic technique to become familiar with all the available knowledge. It aids in stimulating thought and instructs individuals on a variety of topics. The newspaper is one of the most popular reading sources available. Try this exercise right now. Look at the pages of a newspaper or even a magazine. Find some intriguing articles to analyze. Make a list of the fundamental ideas after reading the articles. For instance, consider the relationships between the articles and the themes that each use. Then, comment on the newspaper or magazine's agenda based on what you've read. Whatever sources you like, pick anything that will introduce you to cutting-edge concepts and fresh thinking techniques. Some excellent choices include books about the most successful businesspeople and leaders. To keep your brain in shape, you should read for at least 20 minutes each day.

2. "Tell an Alien." Any theory or piece of knowledge can be used for this task. However, developing your analytical abilities is the major goal here. Find at least 10 theories that you wish to discuss and assess to get started. In this activity, you'll pretend to be an inquisitive extraterrestrial from another planet and ask questions while simultaneously addressing and elaborating on the subjects to yourself. You perform both jobs here, yes. Make sure the topic is simple enough to be comprehended by a space alien. Ask questions about the subjects covered while acting like an extraterrestrial (you can dress up if you wish). For instance, you could start by discussing soccer (where two teams must kick the ball through the goal to score). You can inquire as the alien as to why only two teams are competing or why they must kick the ball.

3. Interactive inquiry. You can maintain mental activity by including critical thinking tasks in your daily life. Make sure to engage in conversations and ask questions if you're attending a lecture, workshop, or training. Asking interactive questions is a fantastic brain-training practice. Additionally, it offers you fresh knowledge that can advance your professional and personal development. Open-ended inquiries are some crucial ones you can ask in general. You may, for instance, ask questions that call for detailed responses rather than simple yes-or-no responses. You must have given your queries careful consideration if they call for additional in-depth responses. That trains your mind to reason more deeply during talks.

4. Develop your arguments. This kind of group discussion exercise encourages critical thinking. The development of your judgment and reasoning abilities is one of the goals. Usually, this is done at institutions and businesses to support the growth of decision-making and critical thinking skills. To organize a debate with your friends or coworkers, use the Barometer Debate. Someone must advocate for the positive position, while the other person must defend the negative position. It's crucial that everyone concerned takes part in the conversation and expresses their ideas. Understanding the definitions of premise and conclusion is crucial when formulating arguments. A premise is a prior assertion from which your conclusion was drawn. The conclusion, or simply the decision reached through reasoning, is the final section of the argument. Every argument has a premise and identifying them is a useful exercise in critical thinking. In the end, you'll need to assess the discussion's flow and comprehend how you arrived at a conclusion. When constructing arguments, good judgment and conclusions are essential.

5. A writing activity. Keep a journal to record your successes and other significant moments. Write down all the significant choices you've made in the past that have advanced your objectives. Determining the major errors that contributed to some of your life's failures is crucial. Analyze your justifications and presumptions, then contrast them with the outcomes. By doing so, you can learn how to make wiser judgments and discover your strengths and limitations, both of which have a significant influence on your degree of success.

Critical thinking is a skill and an art. It needs to be refined and enhanced by regular practice. Long-term, you'll find that you're developing a far higher level of decision-making effectiveness. You will be more likely to achieve more success in all your pursuits if you have a critical mind.

Section 15: Useful Apps

Even though critical thinking is a skill that we all sorely need, schools do not teach it to us often. It is important to come up with novel, out-of-the-box solutions that will provide us with superior outcomes. Here, we have listed five apps that can help improve critical thinking and more.

Lumosity

This is one of the most well-liked apps for fostering creativity and critical thinking, with over 100 million users. Lumosity engages you in learning through interactive gaming, and its exercises will improve your memory, focus, and mental agility. Additionally, it adjusts to your brain's unique strengths and weaknesses. You can pick one of the abilities and deliberately work on it, or you can just complete the tasks of the day. New challenges are constantly added to the app. The creators of Lumosity have also released two more useful apps: Lumosity Mind for meditation and mindfulness, and Figment for developing a creative practice by experimenting with music, art, and writing.

Brilliant

Brilliant is a problem-solving-focused app that substitutes practical learning for lecture videos. Award-winning professors, researchers, and industry experts from MIT, Caltech, Duke, Microsoft, Google, and other institutions created each course. This app is perfect for individuals who want to dive in and master their math, physics, software development, and fundamental logic skills.

MindMeister

With the help of the free mind-mapping tool MindMeister, you may take notes or look for solutions to problems while exploring the logical relationships between various thoughts and themes. It is an excellent tool for visualizing concepts and keeping track of their connections. This prestigious mind map editor is already used by more than 20 million users for ideation, project planning, and other creative tasks. There, you may effortlessly store and manage your ideas. Anytime you feel the amount of information is too much to handle, use a MindMeister or a pen to summarize it.

NeuroNation

NeuroNation is a forerunner in cognitive fitness. More than 30 brain workouts are available from the Free University of Berlin, one of the top universities in Germany. Its primary goals are to enhance memory, develop critical thinking skills, and enhance the quality of life. Even prevention and rehabilitation can be accomplished using NeuroNation. For instance, it asserts that it works well to reduce stress and burnout as well as dementia. With its versatility, it is a helpful tool that never gets boring. The only investment with a 100% return is investing your time in developing your creativity, critical thinking, and brain function. This is particularly true in the context of today's modern world, which encourages creativity and original thought. We should surely appreciate and utilize it for our good because there have never been more opportunities and resources for humanity to grow and improve, all from the convenience of our homes and smartphones.

Shoogar

Shoogar is a daily exercise program that offers 10-minute podcasts to foster creativity. The program employs the Listen-Create-Find Out method, in which you first listen to short tales with original ideas, then come up with your creative solutions for the problems presented, and last learn about the world's top creative instances from organizations and advertising agencies. Shoogar is special and simple to use. Some of the activities also require interaction with surroundings, such as coming up with a catchy name for a wi-fi network or suggestions for ways to foster community among neighbors. When you need to be productive, as when performing a routine, it is unquestionably the finest podcast substitute.

Section 16: The Relation Between Emotions and Critical Thinking

Emotions and critical thinking are part of everyday living. Your ability to manage and regulate your emotions will determine how successful you are in any given circumstance. Regardless of the activity, people must maintain high levels of critical thinking and attention by managing their emotions. Research has shown that our capacity for critical thought is significantly diminished when we are highly emotional. Many of us find ourselves in situations where we must be able to think critically and adjust effectively despite being in highly emotional circumstances. It may be quite helpful to be able to think clearly and strategically while being very emotional. Doing so, however, is very challenging since emotions and critical thinking are inversely correlated; the more strongly we feel something, the harder it is to think critically.

From an evolutionary standpoint, in the past, we required emotional responses to guide us through our complicated social context and to adjust to environmental risks. When a tiger suddenly sprung out at us, when we discovered that our prized food or partners had vanished, or when we consumed tainted food or beverages, emotional reactions helped us cope. We wouldn't be here today if we didn't have emotional responses that enabled us to adjust to those and many other conditions. Or, to be more accurate, those who lacked such emotional reactions were naturally picked out of the gene pool, while those who did were selected to live. We still have that feeling system inside of us even if many of the circumstances from our evolutionary past might not be present now.

Numerous studies from the past two decades have shown that emotions and cognitions are extremely intertwined rather than being separate autonomous systems in our minds and brains. As shown by current brain research, this is true not only psychologically but also neurophysiologically. What we want is to be able to accomplish positive goals in stressful circumstances while still being able to think critically.

The purpose of this book is not to investigate this in depth, but a key piece of advice to follow is that before undertaking any important critical thinking task or decision you make sure to bring yourself in the right emotional state. You can do that also by leveraging your physiology. For example, there have been studies showing that adjustments to our posture and facial expression, adopting so-called power postures or power poses, can have a profound positive impact on our physical, mental, and emotional conditions. This theory comes from the assumption that because of a body–brain feedback loop, how we utilize our body language may alter how we feel. Some benefits can include enhanced energy, increased mood and focus, constructive emotions and ideas, and increased willingness to persevere. Here are some power poses you can try:

- **Powerful Pose:** Place your feet wide apart, your hands on your hips, and look ahead.
- **Empowerment Pose:** Plant your feet firmly, elevate your head and chest, and extend both of your arms with your palms towards the sun. After maintaining this stance for around 60 seconds, it's difficult not to feel full of energy, powerful, and empowered since it's one of the most expansive postures you can adopt in terms of occupying space.
- **Success Pose:** When an athlete wins a race, scores a goal, or achieves any other form of success, you may notice them lifting their hands and arms in celebration over their heads. This is a normal response to

sentiments of triumph and success. If we reconstruct this process and take a stance of triumph, we may then create the same sensations of power and success in the body.

- **Domination Pose:** Locate a nearby table or chair, bend a little forward, and lay your hands on it. This results in a commanding stance that is just a little bit threatening. You can dominate a room and demand respect and attention right away.
- **Mood Boost Pose:** Smiling is one of the best methods to rapidly improve your disposition and self-assurance. Smiling is an example of facial feedback, which holds that changes in facial expression may affect how you feel emotionally. Therefore, your body tells your brain that you are happy when you smile, which can make you feel more at ease and confident.

|Part 2| Logic, Structuring, & Framing

Section 1: 5W2H Analysis to Describe a Problem (Who, What, Where, When, How, How Much)

Have you ever thought about ways to structure problems systematically? The 5W2H Analysis helps you understand your problem, support the problem-solving process, and create more clarity from the beginning.

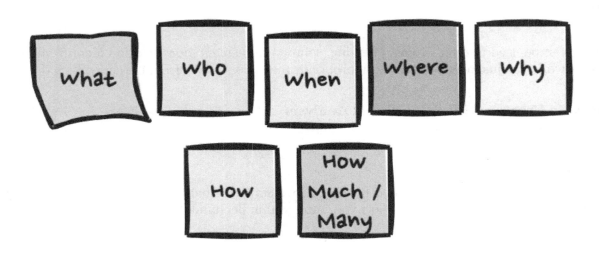

The Concept: 5W2H Analysis

The 5W2H is a problem-structuring technique based on seven key questions: What, Where, When Who, Why, How, and How Much/Many.

W1-What: This is a detailed description of the problem. In other words, the gap between the current situation and the desired situation.

W2-Where: Where is the problem happening? Location, areas? Description and details about the location?

W3-When: When did the problem happen? When did it start? Is it repeating? With what frequency? How long did it last? Did anything else relevant to the problem happen at the same time?

W4-Who: Whom is the problem impacting? Who is suffering because of this problem? Who caused the problem? Who halted the problem? Who is involved with the problem? Who are the stakeholders? Whom should we contact? Who can provide us with more info?

W5-Why: Why is it a problem? Why is this problem important to solve? Why is it urgent? Why must be done? Why did this problem happen?

H1-How: How can we solve the problem? Which alternatives do we have? What process can we follow to solve the problem? How do we organize ourselves to tackle the problem? What steps should we follow? Useful tools may be other frameworks, project plans, and so on.

H2-How Much: What is the size of the problem? How much economic damage is the problem creating? How much is it costing us? How much are we missing? How many people are affected? How many units are affected? How much time would we need to solve the problem?

The **5W2H method** is used in different fields such as:

- business and management,
- crime investigations,
- journalism and reporting,
- scientific research,
- engineering,
- sociology, and
- legal matters.

This method can be used also for project planning, solution implementation, solution identification, and organization of work, you just need to generate appropriate questions starting from the core 5W2H ones.

Tips on How to Create an Effective 5W2H Analysis

To create an effective 5W2H Analysis, follow these steps:

1. Understand and Observe the Situation

Understanding and observing the situation is the first step of a 5W2H Analysis. In this step, you must try to understand how the 5W2H method can support you. After you understand it fully, think about the desired outcome.

2. Create Appropriate 5W2H Questions

Creating an effective analysis using the 5W2H method is very important to identify and define good questions out of the basic root questions (What, Where, When Who, Why, How, How Much/Many). The generated questions must be customized for the problem and context at hand. Sometimes a single root question might lead to many other questions. For example, "why" may state both the reason for the problem and why a conclusion is needed. Following this step will allow you to generate key valuable questions which you could have ignored otherwise.

3. Prioritize and Answer the Questions Properly

Once you have generated the key questions, prioritize and start finding answers for each of them. There might be questions you won't find a straight answer to. If this is the case, create a proper plan for answering such questions. Try to address one question at a time and try to find logical answers to the questions.

4. Execute the Solution

After you complete the 5W2H analysis, create a framework for executing a solution.

Examples

Crime

Situation: A murder has taken place in a nearby townhouse. Mr. Smith has been murdered by an unknown man. There are signs of a knife on his body with severe damage to his right arm. We need to find out who has committed the crime.

What: What is the identikit of the person? What is the identikit of the potential killer?

Who: Who was present during the scene if any? Who has heard anything? Did somebody see something unusual? Who are the people connected to the killed man, family, and friends?

When: When did this happen? What about the time leading to the event?

Where: Where did it happen? Where were the people involved during that time?

Why: Why was this person killed? Why was he alone? Why were other people not there? Why was he there at that time? Why would somebody kill him?

How: How do we organize our investigation? What is our plan? Who does what? How do we communicate about it?

How much: How much time would we need? How many people do we need?

Emergency Situation

Situation: A fire incident took place at 1:00 p.m. in an office building. The authorities of the organization took immediate action. The CFT team has also investigated the cause of the incident by collecting data on the mishap.

What: What has happened? What did the locals say about the incident?

Who: Who were the ones present during the mishap? Who saw it first? Who arrived first for help? Who called the fire brigade? Who notified the police? Who were the members of the electric maintenance team?

When: When did the incident occur? When was the problem first observed?

Where: Where did such an incident happen? Where were the office employees and employers at that time? Where were the local people at that time?

Why: Why did this happen? Why did such a big organization not have proper electrical maintenance?

How: How is the daily electrical maintenance carried out? How must proper care be taken to avoid such mishaps in the future? How could the authorities of the organization be more careful?

How Much: How much attention should the management pay? How much money must be invested for proper electricity maintenance? How many people were affected by the fire outbreak? How many fire extinguishers need to be arranged?

Identifying Non-Conforming Product

Problem: An XYZ company revealed non-conformity sometime after revealing the consignment. After three weeks, the consignment recipient observed wet packaging in the warehouse. Wet cardboard and moisture were discovered in individual packages.

What: What is happening? What else was affected?

Who: Who was the first one to discover the problem? Who reported the problem to the employee in charge?

When: When was the problem first encountered?

Where: Where were these wet packages observed? Where were the wet packages being transported? Where is the company situated?

Why: Why were the products damaged? Why were the packages wet?

How: How did the packages become wet? How do we know that wet packages caused a major problem? After how long was the problem noticed?

How Much: How much loss did the company bear for its damaged products? How many packages were damaged?

Car Failure

Problem: Driving smoothly down a highway, a driver's car engine suddenly stopped. After exiting the vehicle, they also noticed a punctured tire.

What: What is the cause of this trouble? What was the situation after that?

Who: Who was driving the car? Who was inside the car? Who replaced the tire? Who took the car to the garage for repair? Who noticed the trouble first?

When: When did it happen? When did the mechanic show up?

Where: Where did the car stop? Was it on the main road or a highway? Where were the local people? Where were the traffic guards for help?

Why: Why did this happen?

How: How did both engine failure and tire puncture occur at the same time? How long did it take to repair?

How Much: How much did the repair cost? How many people helped solve the issue? How much was the car affected?

Technical Failure

Problem: Several people in a building complain that the lift of the building is slow and frequently breaks down. The budget is too low to undergo a full-fledged repair.

What: What is the name of the company that made the lift? What is the reaction of the authority to the complaints of the people? What can be done while keeping in mind the major problem of running short of budget?

Who: Who were the ones who complained? Who noticed it first? Who reported the concerned authorities for taking a step? Who are the ones using the lift very often? Who are the ones who don't need a lift? Who are the ones using only the staircase and not the lift?

When: When did the lift become slow? When did the budget go down? When did the lift last stop working?

Where: Where is the building located? Where is the lift located in the building?

Why: Why did the lift suddenly become slow? Why does it stop working very often? Why is the budget low? Why can't the lift be repaired soon?

How: How old is the lift? How old is the building? How do such things happen?

How Much: How much is the current budget in hand? How much is required for a proper repair? How many lifts are there? How many people need to contribute to the lift repair?

Loss in Business

Problem: An ABC restaurant is undergoing a great loss since the last year as they are facing a lack of customers.

What: What type of restaurant, is it veg/non-veg? Is it a café, bar, or family restaurant? What are the best-selling dish food items in this place? What can be done for attracting customers?

Who: Who is the owner of the restaurant? Who are the chefs? Who looks after the day-to-day work of the waiters and chefs? Who keeps the accounts?

When: When did the number of customers start declining? When was this restaurant formed? When does this restaurant close and open?

Where: Where is the restaurant located? Where are other good restaurants in the city?

Why: Why has such a thing been seen recently?

How: How does this problem of fewer customers happen? Did they change the chefs? Was the same food quality not maintained?

How Much: How much are current sales? How much were previous sales? How much of the sales are generated on special days and regular days?

Try it out

Think of some problem you know and try using the 5W2H methods to raise insightful questions that can help in the understanding and resolution of the problem. As you may have noticed in the examples above, the 5W2H is useful to get you started, though it does not solve the problem and the questions can be interpreted in different ways. Nevertheless, is a very powerful tool to get you started.

Advantages of Using the 5W2H Method

This method:
• Is quite generic and can be applied to any situation or problem;
• Requires basic sense and no training; and
• Is comprehensive and can address several aspects of a problem.

Disadvantages of Using the 5W2H Method

The 5W2H method may, however:
• Leave answers to most of the questions unknown;
• Be confusing since the same question might have many answers;
• Not be applicable in certain situations, especially those out of your control; and

• Be too broad to raise only important questions, which is why prioritization remains an important step.

Takeaways

The 5W2H method is an effective tool that can help you structure problems and gather general information in a much faster way. So, you can generate good questions and identify the right paths of analysis. This is one of the most basic frameworks for structuring problems in an efficient manner. Try to apply this method to structure your problems or opportunities!

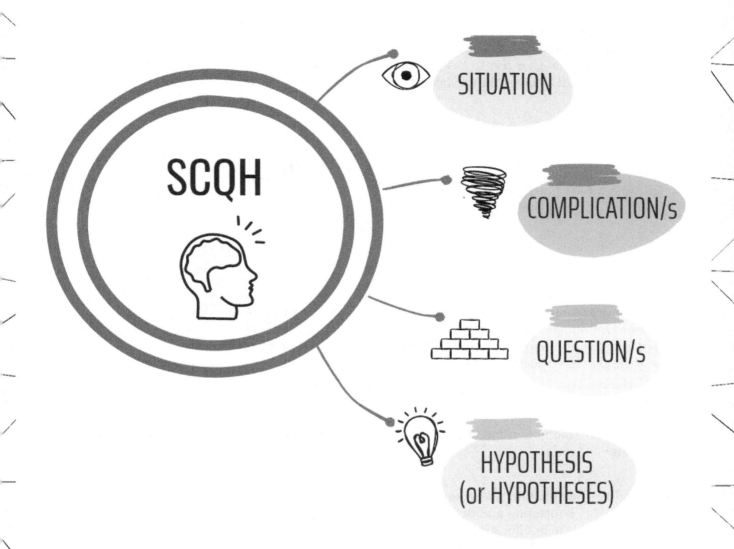

Definition of SCQH

SCQH stands for situation, complication, question, and hypothesis. It is a powerful yet simple tool for structuring problems. It is also useful for storytelling, outlining presentations, and planning projects. SCQH is at times written as SCQA for situation, complications, question, and answer. However, you must treat the last part as a hypothesis instead of an answer so it can be well tested. The main aim of SCHQ is to:

1) Provide a clear understanding of the problem; and
2) Give a clear direction toward finding a solution.

Parts of an SCQH

An SCQH consists of four parts:

1. Situation: This refers to the context and setting of the problem. The situation is like a problem statement. It is a precise description of an issue that has occurred and which needs improvement. The situation comes first when you are solving any problem and guides the direction of your analysis of a problem.

2. Complication: This indicates what the problem is about and what things are not working. The main aim of complication is to build a clear picture of the problem. This also helps you understand the size of the problem. Complications give rise to many questions. In this part, while you can also leverage the 5W2H framework, you should focus on the gap between the current state and the desired state.

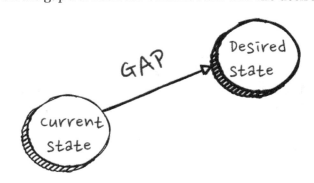

3. Question: The question is the natural reaction a person might have once they listen to the situation and complication. An understanding of the problem is essential to the problem-solving process. Any questions generated from the situation and complication may themselves be problems. You may choose to solve only one or a few of the generated questions. Next, try to find the solutions to the questions in the form of a hypothesis.

4. Hypothesis: Hypotheses are the several assumptions or proposals for solving a question. The hypothesis can be seen as a prediction of the most probable answer to the question at hand. The hypothesis is a very important step in solving any problem. It gives direction and brings focus. A hypothesis must be precise, not vague. For ease of comprehension, a hypothesis can be formulated as a true statement or as a question—whatever suits you better!

Understanding the situation and complications is the first step in recognizing a problem. It helps you understand what is happening and define the problem—the gap between the current state and the desired state. The next step is to ask questions related to the problem, which helps you frame the hypothesis. Finding out the several answers to the questions is what we call developing a hypothesis. The hypothesis is not the final solution to the problem but it is an assumption made to find the solution.

Examples

Business Loss

Situation: We are a soap- and detergent-making company and we have been losing money since 2020. Loss is up to $100k per year.

Complication: If we continue losing money at this rate, we will face bankruptcy very soon. Moreover, we have no new product ready in hand to alter the crisis. (Current state: Business is losing money. Desired state: Business will be profitable again.)

Question: Why is the business losing money? What can we do about it?

Hypothesis (HP):

HP1: Revenues have decreased

    HP1.1 A new competitor has entered the market

HP2: Our base costs have increased

    HP2.2: Cost of raw materials has increased

University

Situation: ABC university is a successful government university that has worldwide recognition. The university has a growing number of students due to its academic excellence.

Complication: Despite the university's success, the state government is facing budget challenges. The government is making cuts across the board. The university needs to find a way for closing this gap within one year. (Current state: Not enough funding to cover expenses. Desired state: Find enough funding to cover expenses.)

Question: What can the university do to cover the missing funding?

Hypothesis (HP):

HP1: Can the university reduce its costs for covering the budget?

HP2: Can the university increase or introduce tuition for some classes?

HP3: Does the government have other funding options?

HP4: Can third parties (e.g., businesses) help by sponsoring some classes?

Steel Supplies

Situation: A steel supplier is selling and producing fewer steel bars. It is currently selling 55% of the total production capacity.

Complication: Due to capacity constraints, the business is turning down orders.

Questions: Why is the plant running at 55% capacity? Can we increase the production capacity? What are the effects of this situation?

Hypothesis (HP):

HP1: Lack of raw material.

HP2: Old production plant with the malfunctioning element.

HP3: Lack of personnel and manpower.

HP4: Power problem.

HP5: Production lines are not balanced.

HP5: Warehousing problem.

City

Situation: Melbourne has a cultural and creative offer. In 2015, 10 million international and Australian visitors visited the city. Creative industries and cultural visitors add to the economic benefits. So, cultural tourism must be grown further.

Complication: Most of what leaders and art agencies have to offer to city culture is not well articulated. Modern art galleries, museums, and galleries are losing visitors. Workshops, exhibition spaces, and studios are declining in the city.

Question: Why is Melbourne experiencing a declining number of visitors? How Melbourne can reverse the trend?

Hypothesis:

HP1: Something happened with the reputation of the city.

HP2: It has become too expensive to access.

HP3: It has become more difficult to navigate around the city.

HP4: Promotion for the city has decreased and is not enough.

HP5: The city lost some key attractions it had before.

HP6: Other cities have more to offer.

HP7: Transportation to reach the city is complicated or there is not enough availability.

HP8: Accommodations are too expensive.

HP9: Something is happening country-wide or worldwide.

Takeaways

The SCQH approach is a great tool for your problem-solving arsenal. By using this tool, you can form a clear view of the situation and its complications. This method helps frame related questions and create hypotheses. These hypotheses will direct your focus and lead to finding a solution to your problem. The next step is hypothesis testing, where you validate, prove, disprove, and/or refine your hypothesis and gain as many learnings as possible.

Section 3: MECE Principle & Synthesis

Intro to MECE

MECE stands for Mutually Exclusive and Collectively Exhaustive. It is a foundational idea in structuring problems. This principle is something to keep in mind when breaking down a problem into smaller pieces, categorizing elements, grouping ideas, solutions, and so on. What does it mean:

1) Mutually Exclusive means that each item can only fit into one category at a time, with no overlaps. Mutually exclusive is derived from the probability theory. This theory states that two events cannot occur at the same time. For example, if you roll a die, the outcome of getting a three or a six are mutually exclusive. Similarly, you can apply the same concept to problem-solving. Mutually exclusive ideas are not overlapping, they are separate.

2) Collectively Exhaustive means that the collection of all the items represents 100% or close to 100% of the elements, nothing must be left out. In other words, this means that the ideas include all the possible options. If you go back to the example of the dice, the set {1,2,3,4,5,6} is collectively exhaustive as well as mutually exclusive.

The MECE principle helps you create a sound structure to break down your problem and helps not leave any important element out.

Alongside the MECE principle is the process of synthesis, a term used to group elements together. Synthesis means taking information and summarizing it into a category of a higher level. You may wonder what the benefit of doing such a categorization is. Forming categories will help you remember easily and help you convey your message to an audience much more clearly.

In the same way, in the case of a business organization, a CEO will look at specific actions rather than at a long list. For example, he needs to focus on improving work culture and capital. This will be easier for him to remember and will help him delve deeper into the specifics and details later. Let's see some examples!

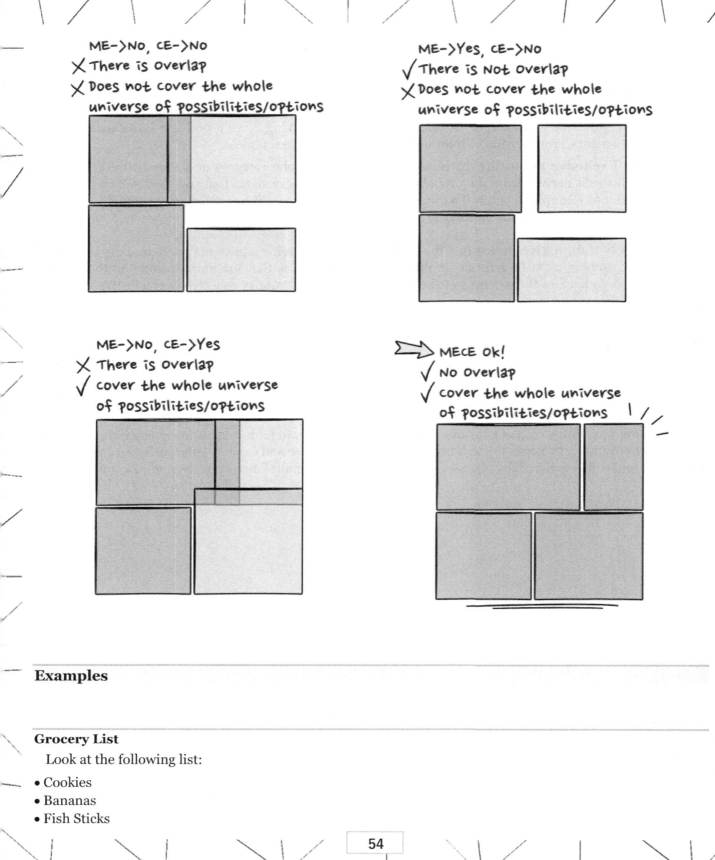

ME->NO, CE->NO
X There is Overlap
X Does not cover the whole universe of possibilities/options

ME->Yes, CE->NO
√ There is Not Overlap
X Does not cover the whole universe of possibilities/options

ME->NO, CE->Yes
X There is Overlap
√ cover the whole universe of possibilities/options

MECE Ok!
√ No Overlap
√ cover the whole universe of possibilities/options

Examples

Grocery List

Look at the following list:

- Cookies
- Bananas
- Fish Sticks

- Muffins
- Strawberries
- Ice Cream
- Buns
- Cheese
- Apples

Look at this random grocery list within 10 seconds and try to remember all the items on the list. It isn't that easy to keep all the items in your mind. Using the guidance of MECE, we take the list and create mutually exclusive groups:

1. <u>Bakery Items:</u> Cookies, Muffins, Buns
2. <u>Frozen Foods:</u> Fish sticks, Ice Cream, Cheese
3. <u>Fruits:</u> Bananas, Strawberries, Bananas, Apples

These 3 identified groups are distinctly different. So, you can call them mutually exclusive. Moreover, the categorization covers all the items on the list. Hence, you can term such grouping as collectively exhaustive. This process has also included synthesis, which means taking information and summarizing it into a category of a higher level.

Mathematical Expressions

Formula For Profit:

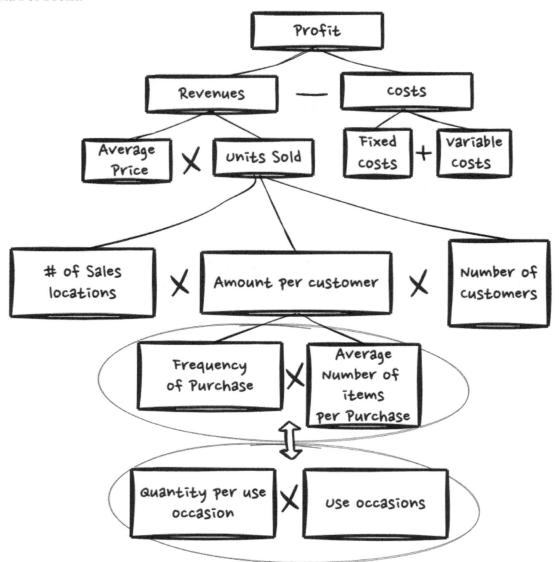

All the parts of these formulas are mutually exclusive and each component is collectively exhaustive because they contain all components driving the profit. If we split more costs into some other components, such as hiring costs, we could use a similar approach while still holding the MECE principle.

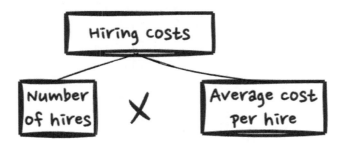

Product Feedback

Let's look at an example of product feedback. We could structure the process as (1) Collecting feedback, (2) Analysis of the feedback, and (3) Action on the feedback. Each step in the process is MECE: distinct (ME) and has no missing steps (CE).

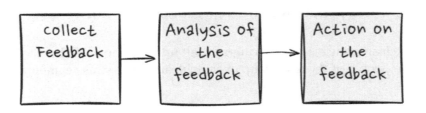

Testing Your Comprehension

Test #1: If we split the world population into song lovers and dance lovers, is this MECE?

This grouping could be CE (collectively exhaustive) but is not ME (mutually exclusive) because many people love both music and dance. Similarly, some people neither love music nor dance. Therefore, this statement is not MECE. Another way to look at it could be as follows i.e. generate 3 or 4 groups, number 3 is a maybe but yes there could be people that do not love music but love to dance!

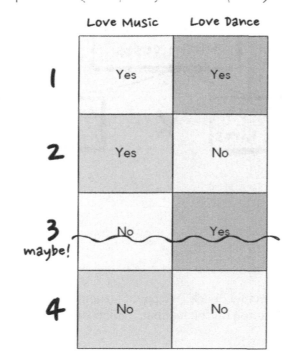

	Love Music	Love Dance
1	Yes	Yes
2	Yes	No
3 maybe!	No	Yes
4	No	No

Test #2: If we split the world population into age groups of 0–20, 21–40, 41–60, and 61–80, is this MECE?

This case is mutually exclusive since a person can only fall under any one of these age groups. However, in the question, there are no people of the age group over 80 years. Thus, this segmentation is not collectively exhaustive.

Test #3: If we split the world population into people over 50kg bodyweight and people under 60kg bodyweight, is this MECE?

In this case, people who have bodyweight between 50–60kg would come under both categories. So, this case is not mutually exclusive. Since the case covers all possible bodyweights, however, it is collectively exhaustive.

Test #4: If we split the world population into people having less than $30,000, between $30,000 and $60,000, and above $60,000, is this MECE?

Since there is no overlap, this categorization is mutually exclusive. This grouping covers all the possible options, so it is collectively exhaustive. Therefore, this case is MECE.

Where Can You Use MECE and Check if You Are Respecting the Principle?

You can use the MECE principle:
- While you simplify a lot of information or data into a smaller set of ideas or groups;
- When you break down a problem into its smaller components;

- When you generate hypotheses;
- While you simplify an article into a small number of high-level categories;
- While organizing a presentation or a summary;
- To break projects down into distinct workstreams; and
- To organize your list of activities.

Takeaways

The MECE principle is a good go-to tool for simplifying or categorizing ideas. It can help you assess whether the information is unclear or organized confusingly. You can use this method to improve your thinking or writing. The MECE principle helps you to think in advance before writing. It can help you design unique frameworks for analysis and problem-solving. Give it a try!

Section 4: The 80/20 Rule

The 80/20 rule was discovered by Vilfredo Federico Damaso Pareto. This rule is also referred to as the Pareto Principle. Vilfredo Pareto (an Italian Economist) first used and discovered this law in macroeconomics (in 1906). Using this 80/20 rule, he described the wealth distribution in early 20th-century Italy. The first thing that Pareto noticed was that 20% of the pea pods in his garden gave rise to 80% of the peas. He brought this same principle to macroeconomics. He showed that 80% of Italy's wealth was governed by 20% of Italy's population. Dr. Joseph Juran applied the 80/20 rule in the field of business production (in the 1940s). He explained that 80% of defects related to products were caused by 20% of the defects in production. He stated that you can improve the quality of products in a business by using the 80/20 rule. Juran called this "the essential few and the negligible many."

Making it simple, the 80/20 rule states that for any situation, 80% of outputs result from 20% of inputs. 80% of the results come from 20% of the effort. 80% of the effects come from 20% of the causes, and so on. The 80/20 rule occurs everywhere in nature. The implication of this is that, in anything, we should find and focus on the 20% that gives the 80% of the results. This is true for problem-solving and other activities we choose to do in our life.

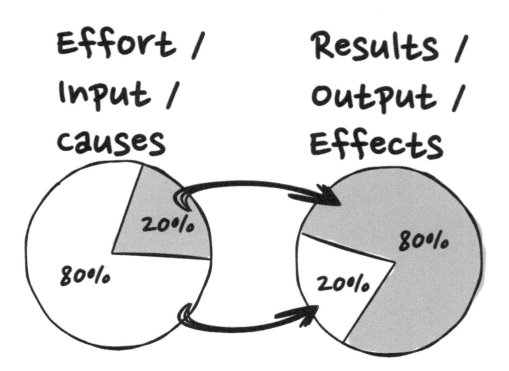

The 80/20 rule can be applied anywhere: Business, economics, personal finance, time management, distribution of wealth, problem-solving, relationships, sports, social issues, and so on.

In business, you may find that 80% of the revenue is produced by 20% of the customers. A company may choose to focus on 20% of the clients since these clients help with generating 80% of revenues. Other business examples include:

- 80% of the total sales are generated by 20% of the sales representatives.
- 80% of total profits are due to 20% of the customer accounts.
- 80% of software crashes are due to 20% of the reported software bugs.
- 80% of health expenditure occurs due to 20% of patients' accounts.

The 80/20 rule can benefit many areas and can help:

- Uplift the results of salespeople;
- Increase daily productivity;
- Make priorities clear;
- Break work down into manageable segments;
- Develop an effective leadership quality;
- Utilize resources efficiently; and
- Develop your problem-solving as well as decision-making skills.

Examples of the 80/20 Rule

Blog Writing

A graduate student, Mary, was working on an assignment on blog writing. The task was to create a blog and track its success within the semester. Mary designed and created a website. The professor evaluated the blogs. Mary's blog generated much less traffic than the blogs of her classmates.

Mary tried the 80/20 rule to solve her issue in her blog writing project. Despite using her time, writing expertise, and technical ability to create her blog she got very little website traffic. Mary now understood that she needs to put more effort into blog marketing.

Deciding to apply the 80/20 rule, Mary asked:

- Which sources consist of the top 20% of traffic in my blog?
- Who are my top 20% audiences to be reached?
- What are the features of this target audience?
- Can I afford more money investment?
- Can I please my top 20% of readers?
- Which blog posts consist of the top 20% of my best-performing topics?
- Can I improve upon those topics and get more traction?

Mary found the answers to these questions, and began editing her blog accordingly:

- She adjusted the design of the blog to address her top 20% target audience.
- She has rewritten the content to meet her target readers.

Mary applied the 80/20 rule in her blog project. Mary understood her audience better and targeted the 20% of the audience that generates 80% of the traffic and reading. She modified the blog's structure and content based on her learning. After these changes, the traffic to her site rose by more than 220%.

Time Management

As per Pareto's principle, being busy is not the same as being productive. Self-employed individuals, entrepreneurs, and small business owners mostly think that working for a long time can produce more results. That is not always true. Thinking with the 80/20 rule in mind, you may find out that 20% of tasks are responsible for the great majority of the results. In this way, you may gain more time to devote to other recreations that you like or generate even more results.

Task Prioritization

1) Find out all your weekly or daily tasks.
2) Find out the major tasks.
3) Which tasks give you more return?
4) Think about how you can manage or reduce the tasks from where you get less return.
5) Use 80/20 to assign priority to the projects you're working on.
6) Plan to focus on tasks that give the most results.

Business Management

While managing a project or a business team, 20% of the people involved in a task may complete 80% of the work. You can use the Pareto analysis to find the most productive workers. Assign the most important tasks to these workers. Make them leaders or guides so they can train others using a similar approach. Interview and observe such team members to find out the unique skills, habits, and qualities that result in their productivity. Use the same knowledge to train other staff members. This will surely improve the productivity of the entire team.

Relationships

You can look at the relationships you have with your group of friends. Now, decide which 20% of your friends are the best, and who supports you in every aspect. If you spend 80% of your time with this 20% of your friends, you will probably feel better.

You can apply the 80/20 rule in building a good relationship with your partner or spouse. You need to understand that 80% of the problems between couples are due to 20% of their behaviors or actions. You must find out the main causes behind the 20% of your behaviors that lead to conflicts or misunderstandings and focus on improving them.

Goal Setting

Applying the Pareto Principle for setting SMART (Specific, Measurable, Achievable, Relevant, Time-bound) goals will increase your productivity overall. First, write down 10 goals on a piece of paper. Then ask yourself: Which goal can have the most positive impact on my life? Which goal on the list can be accomplished today? After you complete this exercise, find the 20% of your goals that will be most valuable. You should keep working on those goals that you've chosen as the most important.

Sales

Ros is the highest-paid commission professional in the US. He wants to double his income over the next 3–5 years, so he used the 80/20 rule on his customer base. He found out that 80% of the profits were generated by 20% of his clients. He also observed that the time spent on a high-profit client was the same as the time spent on a low-profit client. He set up a profile of his top clients and searched for the clients in the market who fit that profile.

Section 5: Top-Down and Bottom-Up Approach

The top-down and bottom-up approaches are methods used for structuring and solving problems. These two terms are often found in business, economics, finance, investing, critical thinking, and sociology. Since the two approaches are similar, many people get confused. As outlined previously, the top-down approach moves from a general issue to a specific issue while the bottom-up approach moves from a specific issue to a general issue.

Top-Down Approach

The top-down approach involves a comprehensive question or theme also known as the governing thought. From this governing thought, you need to break down the problem and identify and develop the next-level elements. In particular, we focus on a small number of significant influencers. Only after these key elements are established, the focus shifts to the level below. This process is repeated to add more levels down the tree.

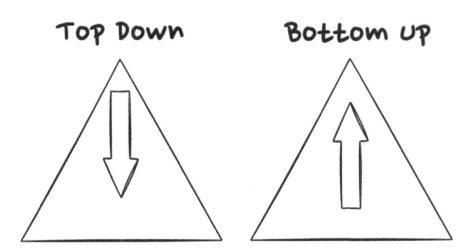

Bottom-Up Approach

The bottom-up approach is the reverse of a top-down approach. It begins with small and specific details. In this approach, the work is focused on a list of issues, then organized into buckets or groups. The process is repeated and many levels are added up the tree. The process continues until one reaches the influencers and governing thoughts.

Section 6: Logic/Issue Trees (Defining Structures, Grouping, and Logical Orders)

What Is an Issue/Logic Tree?

When solving problems, a logic tree is a fantastic tool to use. We will refer to logic trees or issue trees interchangeably. A logic or issue tree is a visual tool that is useful for coming up with a wide range of alternatives. The secret to creating an effective logic tree is to split the problem into its key components. Creating a logic tree is really about categorization, creating logical order, grouping, and layering (going down into the issue and representing it with several layers). A logic tree, beyond being a visual representation of the parts of a problem, is also a useful tool to identify a hypothesis.

Let's create a logic tree by trying to structure a problem. Let's consider this question: "How can I reach more people with my content?" We could use the following logic tree to structure the problem.

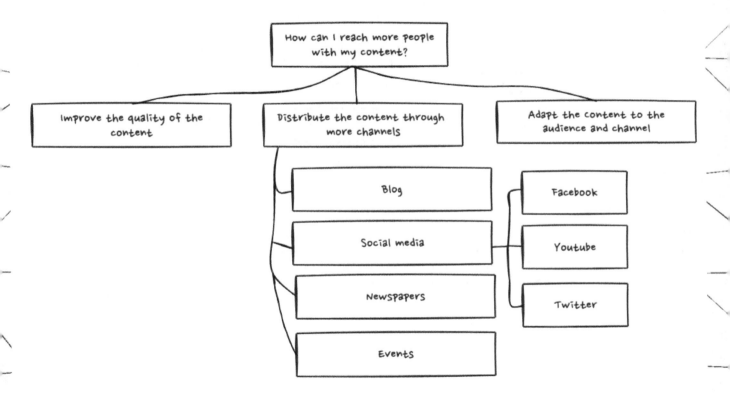

Find more examples in the following section.

Examples of Issue Trees

Buying a Laptop

With the help of a logic tree, you could lay out many options to save money for buying a laptop.

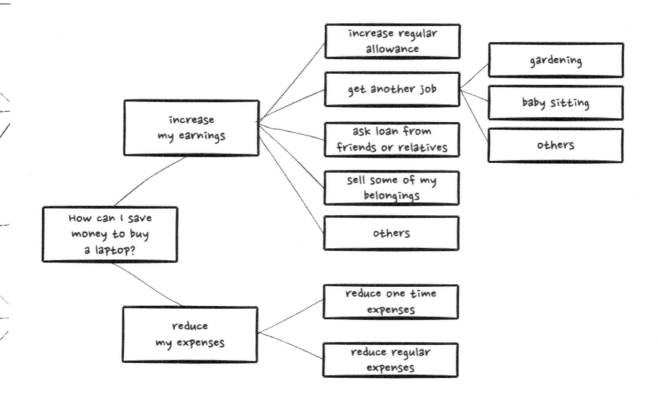

Who took my purse?

Someone stole Mia's purse and she is worried about who has stolen it. She noticed it while she was in her classroom. With the help of this logic tree, Mia can identify many options about who has stolen her purse. She can go through the set of branches and make out who took it and measure whether it is her fault.

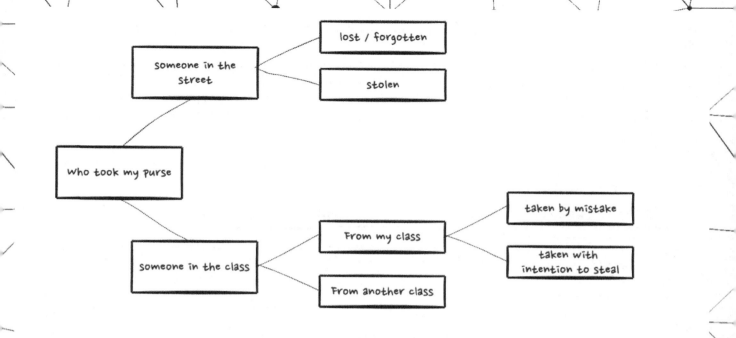

Try Your Own

Take one of the above problems or pick a topic of your choice and develop a logic tree! Remember that the branches formed at each stage must be MECE (mutually exclusive and collectively exhaustive). No branches should overlap with each other, and they should only appear once. Also, remember to apply the principles of logical order and grouping.

How to Structure and Break Down a Problem into its Key Components Through Logic Trees

Possibly the most important aspect of logic is to break down, chunk, or structure a problem into its parts and connect and organize ideas. But what approaches can we use for that? Here is where the process of defining a logical order comes in handy. The most useful way to break down and organize a problem is by using 1) **Time Structures**, 2) **System Structures**, 3) **Classification/Category Structures**, and 4) **Deductive Structures/Orders**. Let's see them one by one.

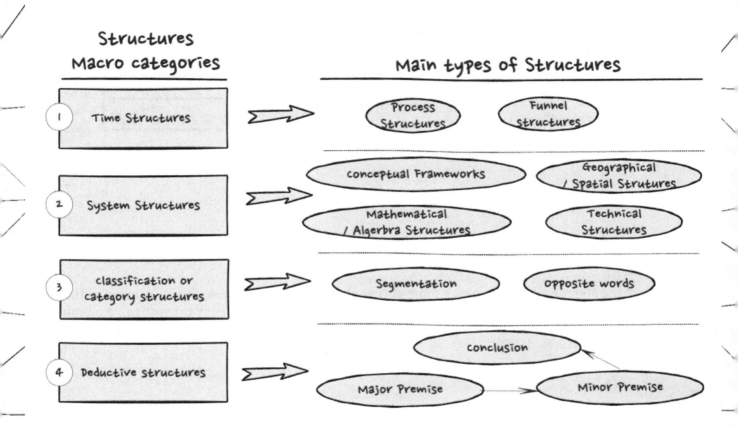

Method 1—Time Structures

Here, problems or ideas are organized or chunked in chronological order. You can use it as a grouping methodology by putting elements that happen during the same time or have similar duration together.

Example of Process 1

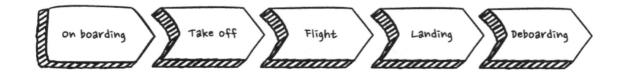

Example of Process 2

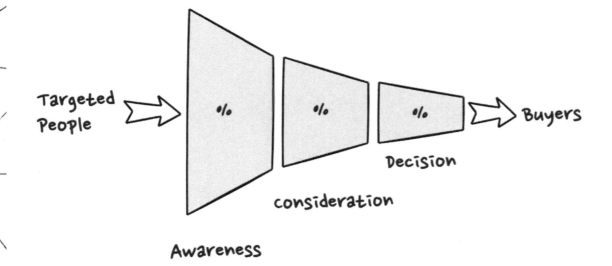

Method 2—System Structures

This method requires your mind to refer to a structure, visualize it, and divide the structure into its parts. The parts must be MECE, you can then group things belonging to specific parts together. An example of a structure could be a map, a framework, a conceptual map, or a technical system.

Example of Conceptual Framework

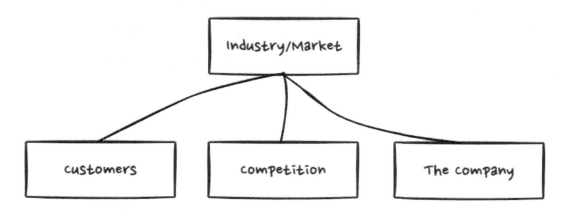

Example of Mathematical Structure (as explained earlier)

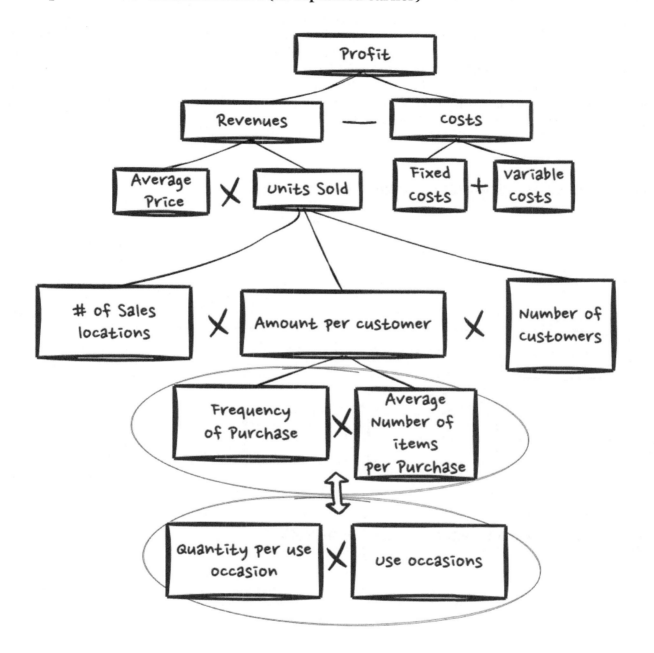

Other Examples of System Structures

- People Process Systems
- Trust = Credibility + Reliability + Intimacy + Self Orientation

Method 3—Classification or Category Structures

In this case, the aim is to group things based on common attributes or characteristics. For example, let's consider you are grouping things based on a hypothetical size. List them from the biggest to the smallest. You then could go up one level and create classes, for example, Class 1 (size 1–3), Class 2 (size 3–6), and Class 3 (size 7–10). You can now group things and, within each class, order them by size as well. The order you use to list groups could be based on how important one idea, thing, or element is compared to another considering a chosen variable. Now is your turn to choose something, find out the common characteristic attributes, form classes, and order them by the chosen dimension.

Example of Age and Geographical Segmentation

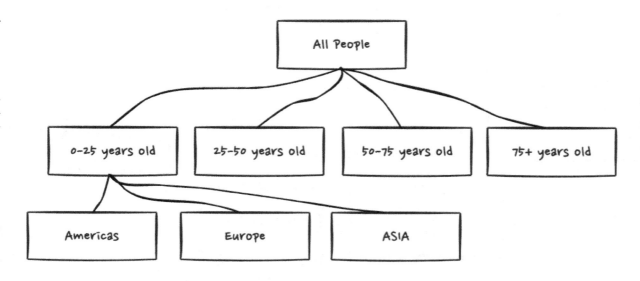

Examples of Opposite Words Grouping and Ordering

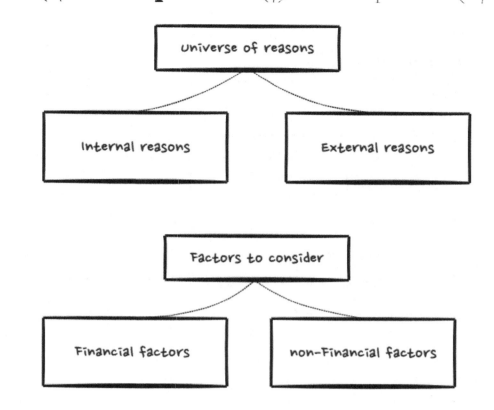

Other examples of opposite words structures could be:

- Supply and demand.
- Short-term and long-term.
- Buy and sell.

Method 4—Deductive Structures/Orders

This method uses instead the order of a logical argument major premise, minor premise, and conclusion. A classic example is the following:

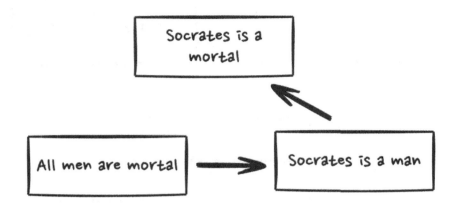

Mixing and Layering

The four methods explained in this section can be applied in combination or alone, but at least one of the methods needs to be used while structuring, grouping, and ordering ideas. This will allow getting as close as possible to a MECE structure. The high-level 3-step process is:

1. Utilize one of the four ways to be MECE to break down the initial layer of the logic tree.
2. Break down the elements of the 1st layer using one of the four methods.
3. Continue to break down the problem through the issues tree as needed with a second, third, fourth layer, and so on.

Finally, remember to leverage the 80/20 rule as well when structuring and solving the problem.

The Only Four Types of Issue Trees That Really Exist

People often wonder how many types of logic/issue trees exist. The answer is simple, there are four types. The most important are 1) Descriptive Issue Trees, 2) Diagnostic Issue Trees (aka Problem or WHY trees), and 3) Solution Issue Trees (aka How Trees). Data and facts that would support the why and how are then needed to prove the hypothesis generated by using trees of type 2 (Diagnostic Trees) and type 3 (Solution Trees). The type-4 tree is less important but encompasses the answering of all other types of questions beyond why and how. This tree includes the answering of questions such as where/when/who/what.

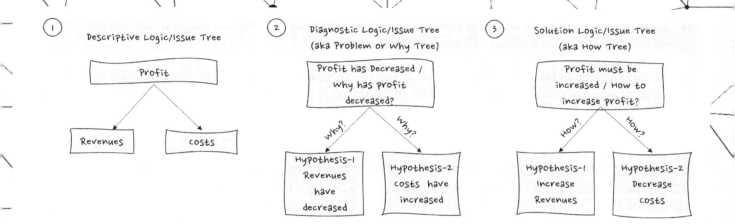

1—Descriptive Trees

Descriptive Issue trees, sometimes simply referred to as logic trees, describe the core components of a problem. For example, the formula [Profit = Revenues – Cost] is an example of a descriptive tree.

However, if we specify the problem or objective e.g. why profit is declining then you can state a more specific tree and hypotheses such as because *hypothesis-1)revenues are decreasing* and/or *hypotheses-2)cost are increasing*, this gives you a Diagnostic Tree (aka Problem or Why Tree). If the question/problem is how can we increase profit then you can state an issue tree as by *hypothesis-1)increasing revenues* and/or *hypothesis-2)decreasing cost*, this gives you a Solution Tree (aka How Tree).

2—Diagnostic Trees (aka Problem or Why Trees)

Diagnostic Trees, also known as Problem or Why Trees, determine why a problem is happening. It helps you create your own hypotheses on the possible causes of the problem. Retaking the example from before, if you ask "why is profit declining," you may come up with hypotheses such as 1)revenues are decreasing and/or 2) costs are increasing.

3—Solution Trees (aka How Trees)

Solution Trees or How Trees help determine the possible solutions to a problem. From there, you can determine which are the most effective in solving the problem. You can hypothesize as many solutions but you must make sure that those are reasonable and relevant to the problem.

Following the previous example, if you instead ask "how can we increase profit," then you can hypothesize HP-1)increasing revenues and/or HP-2)decreasing cost.

5 Rules to Follow While Working With Issue/Logic Trees

When working with Issue/Logic Trees, it is good practice to remember to:

1) State your hypotheses clearly when you construct your tree;
2) Start your analysis in one branch of the tree that has more potential to bring you to the root cause of the problem or to the solution of your problem;

3) Go deeper into a branch, adding a new level down the tree (Mixing and Layering) if data suggest so, or go up one level and work on a different branch of the tree;

4) Refine the hypotheses while you uncover new insights; and

5) Use comparison and benchmark in your analysis, i.e., compare data to the past (trend, pattern, current year vs. previous year, current month vs. previous month) and to external (if you analyze a company you could compare it to its competitors).

How Many Buckets Should You Have in Every Layer of an Issue/Logic Tree?

Short-term memory (STM) is a term proposed by Atkinson-Shiffrin. According to them, the STM has a capacity of about 7 items and a duration between 15–30 seconds. Most adults can store 5–9 items in their short-term memory. The idea of the magic number 7 was introduced by Miller in 1956. It is thought that adults can hold 7 plus or minus 2 items in their short-term memory. In Miller's theory, he performed a digit span test using every number and letter, except the number 7 and the letter W. This is because 7 and W have two syllables. He noticed that it was easier for people to recall numbers rather than letters. The average recall for numbers was 9.3 and 7.3 for letters. The process of rehearsal, of course, helps keep items in short-term memory. This can be done through acoustic encoding—verbally repeating the items. The structuring process in your problem-solving should use between 3 and 7 groups because it is easier to manage and remember them. For example, you can create a 7-step process, 3 key points, 5 hypotheses, and so on. This does not mean you cannot have more, but you should aim to create groups and a hierarchical level.

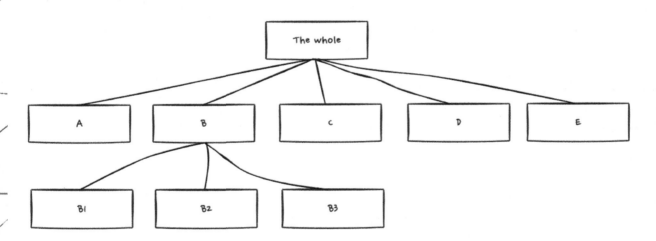

Benefits of Using Logic Trees

Among the several benefits of learning and using Issue/Logic Trees we can highlight four:

1) Issue Trees thoroughly represent a problem in is its key parts.

2) Issue Trees help elegantly divide problems so each part can be tackled independently.

3) Issue Trees will help you have a complete list of potential hypotheses or root causes of the problem and be MECE.

4) Issue Trees will help you prioritize (which we will expand on later).

Section 7: Logic Flow Trees, Decision Trees, and Yes/No Trees

A Logic Flow Tree, also called Logic Flow Diagram, is a graphical representation of a process, be it a decision process, a technical process, a business process, or otherwise. Logic Flow Diagrams can be used to:

• Structure a decision,
• Investigate a problem,
• Gain knowledge of how a process is structured, and
• Explain to others how a procedure is carried out.

The elements of a logic flow diagram are as follows:

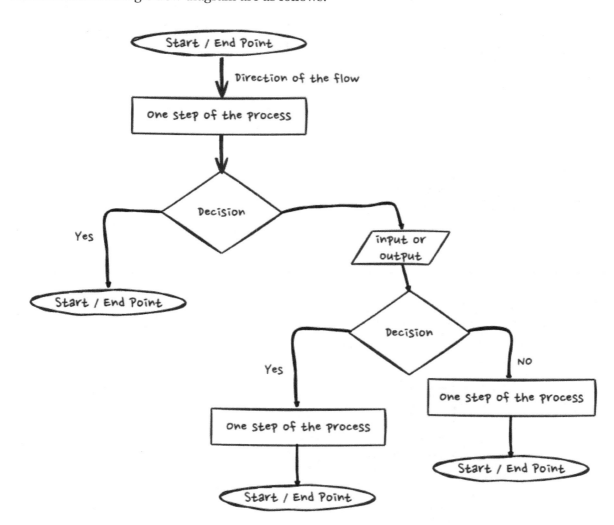

If you reduce the Logic Flow Diagram to only Decisions, you reduce it to a Decision Tree. Further, if the decisions are only Yes/No, it becomes a Yes/No Tree.

Let's make it practical with one example: "Should you change your job?"

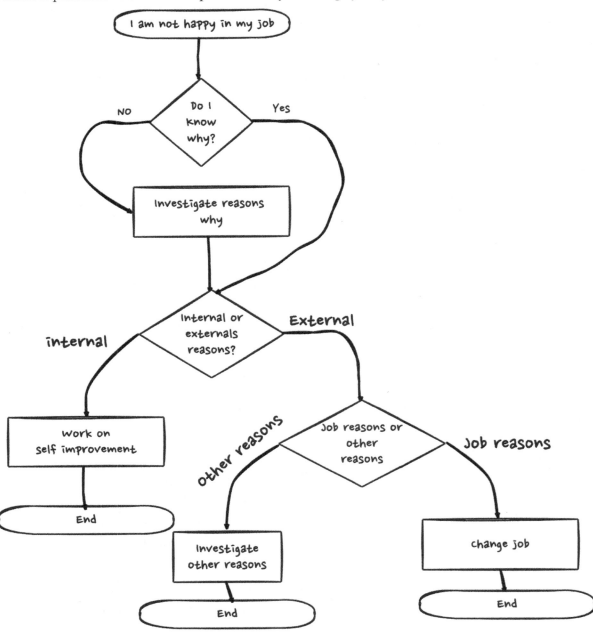

The example above is a simplification, but it is to give you an idea of how you can have fun by using Logic Flow Trees, you can create your own version of it, something that makes more sense to you. Use Logic Flow Trees to help you be more rational and structure better problems, decisions, or solutions.

For fun, if you know the "The Big Bang Theory" series, you can google "The Friendship Algorithm Sheldon Cooper" to see how the flow diagram was used by Sheldon to help him make new friends!

|Part 3| Problem-Solving

Section 1: Problem-Solving Definition and Process

Everyone has problems to solve. Whether it is with family, friendships, work, or school, people have their fair share of challenges. Unfortunately, only a few were taught how to face these problems properly and efficiently. When people face challenging tasks, they often run away from them or pass the responsibility onto another person. Little do they know that they're missing out on an opportunity to learn, grow, get good grades, get promoted, or better their life. Wouldn't you be upset if you found that the challenge you passed up was your ticket to success?

Many people deflect from problems. They always want to stay inside their comfort zone. However, comfort zones do not offer growth and opportunity. It makes you stagnant because you don't improve yourself. Facing a problem will spark your creativity and your wit. It allows you to enhance your emotional and intellectual prowess, making you stronger and wiser. Wouldn't it be great to challenge yourself occasionally, set a goal, and take one step at a time to accomplish it? I guarantee that after you start solving problems systematically, you will feel better about yourself. You'll be happy with the lessons you learned. Then, you will be ready to take on another challenge.

So, what is problem-solving anyway? First, let's define a **problem**: a problem can be defined as *the **gap** between a Current Undesired Situation/State and the Desired Situation/State*. **Problem-solving** is finding a way or ways to get from the current undesired state to a future desired state. This encompasses stages such as defining and understanding the current situation, determining the cause/s, identifying, prioritizing, and selecting alternatives, and implementing one or a set of solution/s. Problem-solving is a practical skill that everyone should learn and build. It not only helps people achieve their goals and earn opportunities, but it also paves the way for learning and resilience. The problem-solving process can be broken down into eight steps:

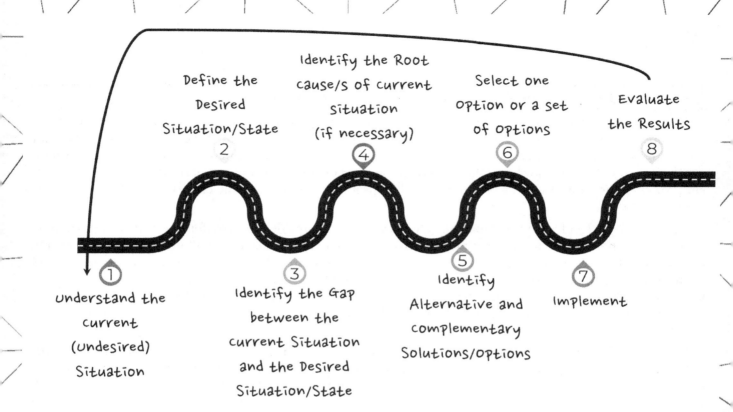

1) Understand the Current (Undesired) Situation. This first step entails defining the problem. What is happening now? Who is affected? How are they affected? If possible, note everything to make sure that you consider every detail. Note what is not working. Include what is lacking.

2) Define the Desired Situation/State. What should happen? What should the situation look like, and how should things be working? During this phase, think outside the box. Do not limit yourself to only a few possibilities. Widen your imagination and be more creative.

3) Identify the Gap Between the Current Situation and the Desired Situation/State. After you define the desired state, you also need to determine the gap between the current situation and the desired situation. This should be as measurable as possible.

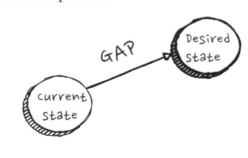

4) Identify the Root Cause(s) of the Current Situation (If Necessary). To support you in finding the root causes, you could use the *Diagnostic Trees* discussed previously. Do not limit yourself to only one reason since there may be many co-existing causes. As much as possible, have data and facts that support your conclusion.

5) Identify Alternative and Complementary Solutions/Options. Brainstorm what you need to do to address the root cause and narrow the gap between your current undesired state and your desired state. Be as creative and impractical as possible to exhaust as many ideas as you can.

6) Select One Option or a Set of Options that allows going from the current state to the desired state. Remember to prioritize the options. You can use one or some of the methods listed in the following sections to help you choose between the options.

7) Implement. During this phase, you will now activate the solution/s that you chose, for which there will be two phases:

   a) *Action Plan Development*—This phase entails creating a list of action plans. Make sure the solutions are time-bound, practical, measurable, and attainable. This way, you know that you can implement the plan promptly. If you are working in a team, divide the work and clarify who's doing what to make sure that every action is carried out well.

   b) *Execute Action Plan*—Execute the action plan to reach the desired state.

8) Evaluate the Results. Many believe that implementing the solution is the end of the problem-solving method. However, you need to evaluate the results to make sure that the chosen solution is sustainable and effective. Is the solution allowing you to experience your desired state? If not, you may need to repeat the first seven stages.

Following the eight steps explained above, there is an additional one:

Continuously Improve. Once you see that the solution is working, your work doesn't necessarily stop there. You should always put an effort to find improvement in yourself, your team, your family, or your company. This way, you can maximize your results and unleash your full potential.

Types of Problems

Let's look at some of the most common challenges that you may face.

1) How do we go from the current state to the target state?

This problem type is one of the most common, the current state/situation is clear and desired/target state is clear, as is the gap. The objective is to find solutions on how to go from the current state to the desired state.

2) We have different alternative solutions on how to go from the current state to the target state, which one should we select?

This type of problem happens to everybody. There are many possible solutions to go from the current state to the desired state. For example, you may want to lose weight and there are different alternatives: There's the gym, intermittent fasting, the ketogenic diet, and so on. The problem is picking the best solution or combination of solutions to move from your current situation to your desired situation.

3) Do we have a problem?

Sometimes the problem is understanding if there is an actual problem. We need to understand where we are now and where we want to be and see if there is a considerable difference. This way, we can eventually understand how to get there. In this scenario, the problem solver is unsure if there is a problem to solve. In many cases, people start to solve or fix something that isn't broken. An example would be unnecessary constructions.

Something like this is sometimes seen when governments and companies fix roads, pavements, and buildings that are not broken or worn off. However, because they have the budget, they opt to have them refurbished. While this is a good attempt for improvement, it may be impractical, especially when they should be prioritizing other areas that have more damaged structures. Had they assessed the problem properly they would have seen other projects that should have budget priority.

Section 2: Pros and Cons Assessment

When presented with a challenging decision, many of us experience an "analysis freeze." We frequently spend a lot of time considering all of the options out of fear of making the "wrong" decision, which makes it difficult to come to a decision. Other times, we may make judgments without fully weighing all of our options because we are certain that we already know what the best course of action is.

With the use of the Pros and Cons assessment, we can achieve more confident conclusions. This assessment is a straightforward but powerful decision-making technique that enables one to view the problem from several viewpoints. You are encouraged to approach your decision rationally by using a straightforward pros and cons list rather than using your gut feeling. This technique is also very helpful when making decisions as a group. It can assist your team in coming to a fair, well-informed choice and it encourages each member to take into account various viewpoints.

How to Use It

First, create a two-column grid and put the decision you must choose at the top. Put pros on one side and cons on the other. List all potential advantages of the choice in the pros column and all potential disadvantages in the cons column. Now think about the things you've noted, and give each one a good or bad rating. For instance, you could use the scale below with as much objectivity as you can.

-3	-2	-1	0	1	2	3
Strong CONS	Mild CONS	Light CONS	Neutral	Light PROS	Mild PROS	Strong PROS

Once you're done, compute the total scores in each column, then subtract the total for the pros and the total for the cons. If your total score is positive, you should consider it as a data point for going forward with the option at hand. If you have a suspicion that the solution is incorrect, spend some time locating any potential contributing elements.

Example

Should I take a degree?

Score	PROS Description	Score	CONS Description
+3	New Employment Opportunities	-3	Debt
+1	Build Network with Others	-1	No Guarantee to get a well paid job
+3	Discover New things	-1	Does not prepare for the real world
+7	TOTAL	-5	TOTAL

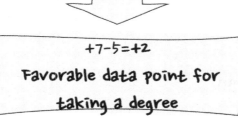

+7-5=+2
Favorable data point for
taking a degree

Section 3: Prioritization Matrices

Prioritization Matrices are good tools to help with prioritizing among a set of options, actions, and so on. They are typically used in a 2x2 format for simplicity but 3x3 can also be used. They offer several advantages, including speed and fast rationalization.

You must choose the terminology that, for your objectives, best fit each axis. Some people make use of the *importance vs. simplicity axes*. Others compare *importance* to *uncertainty*. The Eisenhower Matrix, also known as the *Urgent Important Matrix*, is another matrix type used for prioritization. Prioritization matrices come in numerous variations, but the vertical axis is almost always some variation of More Important vs. Less Important. Finding out the priority is the main objective of these matrices.

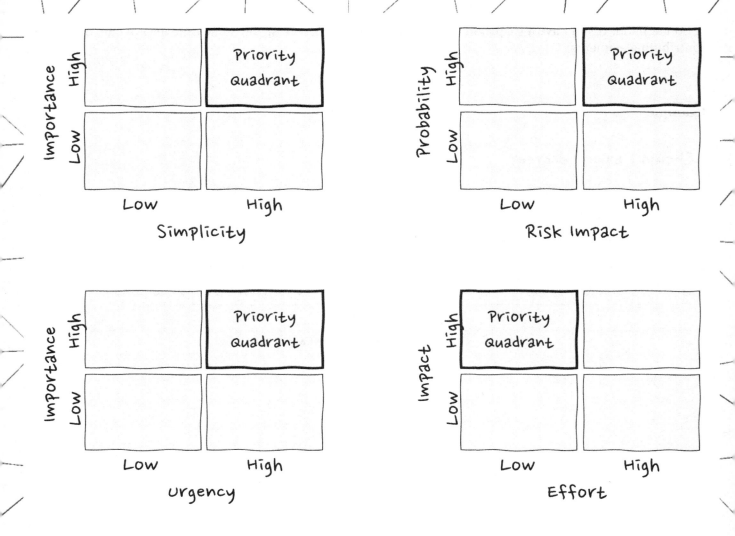

Action Priority Matrix

Actions are placed across effort and impact axes. The way to go about it is to

1) Make a list of the important tasks you want or need to do.
2) Grade these on effort and impact.
3) Arrange the tasks on the Action Priority Matrix per your results.

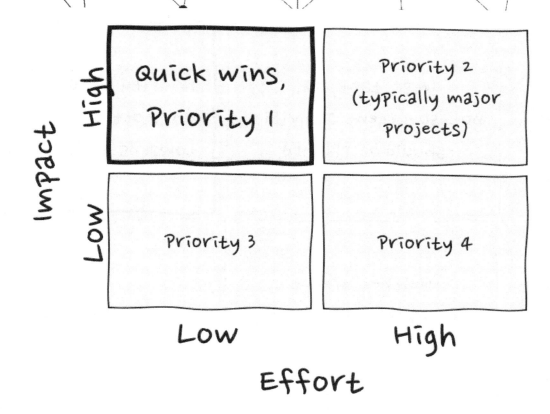

Importance/Urgency aka Eisenhower's Matrix

The Eisenhower Matrix, also known as the Urgent Important Matrix, can help you in selecting and prioritizing activities according to their significance and urgency. It can help you detect less important and urgent jobs that you should either assign to others (delegate) or skip completely.

From 1953 until 1961, Dwight D. Eisenhower served as the 34th President of the United States. He was the Supreme Commander of the Allied Forces during World War II and a general in the US Army before becoming president. Later, he was appointed as NATO's first supreme commander.

Dwight always had to make difficult judgments about which of the several duties he should concentrate on each day. This ultimately inspired him to develop the now-famous Eisenhower principle, which helps us prioritize according to significance and urgency today.

Organizing jobs according to priority and urgency yields four quadrants with various working methods:

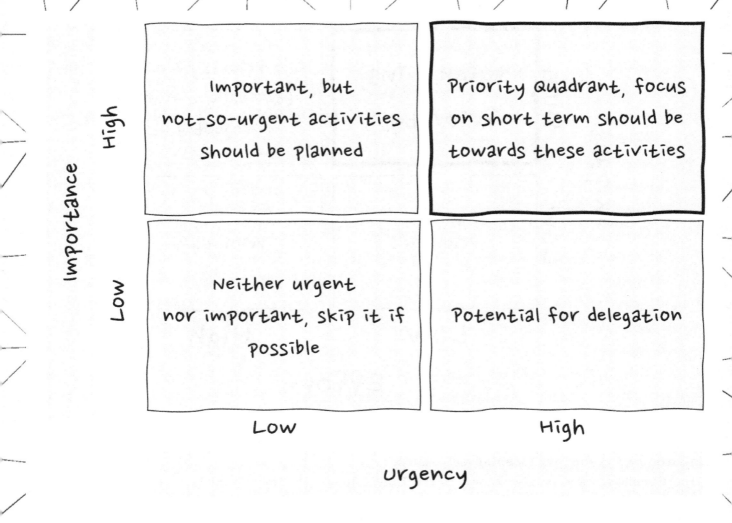

Impact / Probability Matrix

An impact probability matrix is a powerful tool that can be used either for **analyzing risks or opportunities** according to their impact and probability of happening. If we talk about risks, we would refer to it as a *Risk Impact & Probability Matrix*. If we talk about opportunities, we would refer to it as an *Opportunity Impact and Probability Matrix*. But we must first comprehend what impact and probability represent to fully comprehend how this tool functions.

Finding the likelihood that something will materialize is referred to as risk/opportunity probability. A risk/opportunity will be given a score such as 1, 2, or 3, (Low, Mid, High) in terms of its probability of happening.

Impact assessment refers to determining how the risks or opportunities will affect the state of things or the situation if they were to materialize. We should proceed by assigning scores to grade the impact. For a 3x3 matrix, we would have 1, 2, and 3 (low impact, mid impact, high impact).

The Impact Probability matrix displays the likelihood that a risk or opportunity will materialize as well as its potential effects.

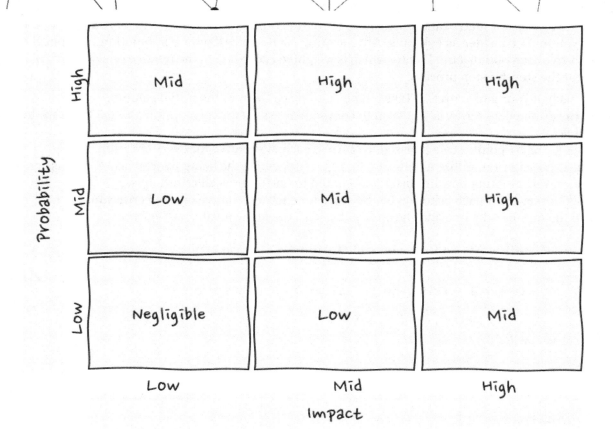

In the top right corner, you will find strong risks or opportunities. In the center are the medium risks or opportunities, and low and negligible risks or opportunities are found in the bottom left corner.

The next conceptual step is to then strategize and define how to address each risk or opportunity given their placement in the matrix. For example, you may choose to:

(R) Resolve, Pursue, or Address the opportunity or risk by minimizing or maximizing the probability and impact, depending on if it is risk or opportunity.

(A) Accept things as they are and take no action.

(T) Transfer the risk or opportunity to a third party. This makes more sense for risk through an insurance mechanism, or in the case of an opportunity that cannot be pursued.

Section 4: Decision Matrix

The Decision Matrix technique was developed by British product designer Stuart Pugh to use mathematics to rank alternatives that have several qualities (dimensions). Making decisions can be aided using a decision matrix, especially when there are many options available and a lot of varied considerations to make. It's a fantastic strategy to apply when making any significant decision where there isn't an apparent preferred alternative. Utilizing a Decision Matrix Analysis enables you to make decisions with confidence when others might be having difficulty doing so.

To execute a decision matrix analysis, you must first arrange your alternatives as rows on a table and the elements you must consider as columns. After scoring each choice/factor combination, you put these scores together to give each option a final score, which is weighted according to the relative relevance of each element. Let's look at the step-by-step process:

1) Define each of your alternatives. Make a table, and place them in the initial column.
2) Select the dimensions/criteria you wish to compare or assess for each option and list them in the first line of your table.
3) Use a 3-, 5-, or 10-points scale to assign a score to each alternative for every criterion.
4) Analyze each criterion, utilize a scale of 1–3, 1–5, 1–10, with 1 the being poorest score, and assign a score to each criterion representing how important compared to one other each criterion is.
5) Multiply the score for each criterion by the score for each alternative on each criterion.
6) Sum all the numbers by line and the alternative with the highest value is the winner!

Assessment/Grading of the Criteria and Options

criteria	criterion 1	criterion 2	criterion 3	...	criterion-N
criteria weight (1–3)	2	3	2	...	1
Option/Alternative 1	3	1	3		1
Option/Alternative 2	2	2	2		3
Option/Alternative 3	1	3	1		1
...					
Option/Alternative N	3	1	3		3

Computation of the Total Score

criteria	criterion 1	criterion 2	criterion 3	...	criterion-N	Total Score
criteria weight (1-3)	(2)	(3)	(2)	...	(1)	n.a.
Option/Alternative 1	(2) x 3 = 6	(3) x 1 = 3	(2) x 3 = 6		(1) x 1 = 1	16
Option/Alternative 2	(2) x 2 = 4	(3) x 2 = 6	(2) x 2 = 4		(1) x 3 = 3	17
Option/Alternative 3	(2) x 1 = 2	(3) x 3 = 9	(2) x 1 = 2		(1) x 1 = 1	14
...						
Option/Alternative N	(2) x 3 = 6	(3) x 1 = 3	(2) x 3 = 6		(1) x 3 = 3	18

In the example above, the alternative N is the one with the highest score and the one that should be chosen. Below is a simple and more concrete example of a possible application for choosing which city to move to. The results of the analysis indicate city 1 as the one with the best score.

criteria	Quality of life	Location	climate	cost of life	Total Score
criteria weight (1-3)	3	2	2	1	n.a.
City 1	3	1	3	3	20
City 2	2	2	2	3	17
City 3	1	3	1	2	13
City 4	2	3	1	2	16

Section 5: Organizing Action With the 5W2H Method

As introduced earlier, the 5W2H method is quite flexible, in addition to framing a problem can also be used as a tool to organize action/s. The 5W2H Method is an excellent technique to ensure that everyone is on the same page and that tasks are completed on time. Using it to put fresh ideas into practice, to implement solutions can be very beneficial.

Ideas have no real value if they aren't put into practice. The 5W2H approach is a terrific resource for getting things started when brainstorming a new course of action, whether you're working alone or in a group.

How to get started? Create a table with seven columns or a list with seven buckets and answer the following questions. You'll be well set to create an effective action plan!

1) What needs to be done?
2) Why should it be done?
3) Where?
4) When must be done?
5) Who will execute it?
6) How, what methods and processes should be followed? Role Models?
7) How much is it going to cost or should it cost?

The "What" section will be filled with the actions you choose, and the "Why" column will be filled with the justifications for your choices. Assign a single person (or "Who") to do each activity. That clarifies responsibility and makes it difficult to pass blame if a work isn't finished on time. Additionally, if you want to prevent procrastination and ad hoc down-prioritization, the time-bound aspect or "When" is crucial. You might also want to try using the RACI matrix to assign responsibilities.

You must decide if you require the "Where" column. If you work from several places geographically, it could be quite helpful, but if you just work from one, it might not be as helpful. Bear in mind, though, that it may also be used to identify preferred partner names or locations where your team will keep records.

You could occasionally leave the field for "How" empty. In that case, will be up to each responsible to define the how. However, it does serve as a useful location to outline any specific procedures you want to be followed or to provide a list of the standards you want people to follow.

The "How much" section could occasionally be left blank as well, though it depends on the magnitude of the solution or project under implementation.

Section 6: RACI Matrix

A responsibility assignment matrix (RAM), often known as a RACI chart or RACI matrix, is a tool used in project management. It's a straightforward table or spreadsheet listing all project stakeholders and their degree of engagement in each activity, indicated by the letters R, A, C, or I. Once these roles are established, tasks may be assigned to them, and work can then start. RACI stands for:

- **(R)—Responsible**. The individual who performs the work, produces the deliverable, or makes a decision. There should be at least one responsible person for each task.
- **(A)—Accountable**. The person or group of people who "own" the work. When the work, goal, or choice is finished, they must provide their approval. This individual is responsible for ensuring that roles are allocated in the matrix for all associated activities. The accountable party in the RACI equation assigns and monitors the project's work. It is their responsibility to ensure that the assigned individual or team is aware of the project's requirements and that the task is finished on schedule. Only one person should be held accountable for each assignment.
- **(C)—Consulted**. People who are consulted offer suggestions and criticism on the project's development. They have a stake in a project's success. Before beginning a task, it's typically necessary to speak with these stakeholders to learn more about their needs. They should also speak with them again as work progresses and after a job is finished to gather feedback on the results.
- **(I)—Informed**. It's important to keep "informed" people updated on a project's status without consulting them or giving them too much information. They must be aware of events because they may have an impact on their work, but they are not involved in making decisions. The informed parties are typically not part of the project team.

How to Structure a RACI Matrix

1) List each job that is necessary to complete the project on the left side of the table, in sequence of completion.
2) List each project stakeholder in alphabetical order along the chart's top.
3) Fill in the cells by stating the role of each person according to the RACI definition (Responsible, Accountable, Consulted, Informed).
4) Make sure at least one stakeholder has the role of responsible and accountable.
5) There should never be more than one stakeholder as Accountable for any task.
6) At the beginning of the project, present, debate, and agree upon the RACI model with your stakeholders. This also entails settling any disputes or uncertainties.

Below an example of a possible use of the RACI matrix.

Tasks	Anna Sales	Jacob Designer	John Research Analyst	Rose Developer	William Architect
Task 1	R	I	A	C	R
Task 2		A	R		C
Task 3	C	A	R	C	I
...					
Task N	I	I	C	R	A

Section 7: How to Leverage Constraints to Be More Creative

For many years, psychologists' prevailing theory was that limitations prevented people from becoming creative. The attractiveness of this argument is clear to anybody who has ever worked in a constricting bureaucracy, dealt with a micromanaging supervisor, or attended a school that teaches to the test. But it does not tell the complete tale.

Patricia Stokes is a psychologist at Columbia University and a specialist in the study of creativity. In one 1993 experiment of hers, rats were made to press a bar using just their right paws. They eventually worked out how to push the bar in more ways than another set of rats that had unrestricted use of their limbs, in addition to learning to adjust to that restriction. This type of creativity, sometimes known as "little c" creativity, focuses on finding novel ways to use existing resources to address real-world issues rather than on creating original creations. And it is this type of inventiveness that frequently receives little attention.

We frequently associate creativity with the arts, with the ability to create works of art. But the fact is that it's a crucial component of finishing simple daily tasks. It's what enables an elementary school teacher to come up with a fun method to teach subtraction, a programmer to write their first line of original code, and a product manager to locate a new market for an existing product. And in some circumstances, these diverse limitations appear to enhance our performance.

In a 2015 research, Ravi Mehta from the University of Illinois and Meng Zhu from Johns Hopkins University investigated how people's creative resource utilization is influenced by their perspective on plenty or scarcity. The researchers reasoned that by drawing attention to resource scarcity, they may weaken people's inclination to make better use of what was at hand. The researchers conducted five experiments to evaluate their hypotheses. Mehta and Zhu concluded that when there is abundance, individuals lack the will to make creative use of their resources.

In other words, our settings either encourage us to view things in a different way or they don't. This suggests that creativity is situational rather than an innate ability or personality attribute. When faced with scarcity, individuals allow themselves the flexibility to use resources in non-traditional ways because they must. A mental capability that would be underutilized otherwise is required by the circumstance. This suggests that having an abundance of resources may not be beneficial. With limitations that force us to make the most of what we have, our issues, difficulties, and challenges may become more bearable. The research indicates that in the absence of limitations, we often recall representative usage scenarios from memory.

With limitations, we focus our mental effort on performing more creatively. You may receive a few good suggestions if you request somebody to propose or construct a product. However, there's a good probability that you'll receive considerably better outcomes if you ask somebody to engineer or construct it while working within a limited budget. Budgets greatly enhanced how resourceful individuals were in reacting to these issues, leading to better solutions. In fact, that's exactly what a group of researchers discovered when they investigated how people develop new things, prepare meals, and mend damaged toys.

Therefore, even though you might not consider a situation where there are limited resources and constraints as positive, you may be surprised to discover that constraints could in fact be a creative hotspot and could pave the way for some unexpected ideas.

|Part 4| Achieving Clear and Effective Communication

Section 1: Organizing Your Communication and Storytelling Techniques

Everyone has a dream—a dream to speak up, a dream to be heard, a dream to be remembered. It's to leave this world with an impact, so generations can remember you and your words. Think about Barack Obama, Oprah Winfrey, Winston Churchill, Nick Vujicic, Brian Tracy, and Jesus Christ—what do they have in common? People remember their sayings. We remember them because at some point they inspired us. Whenever we feel down or demotivated, we turn to their sayings and stories to lift us back up. All of these people have unique things to say and, depending on your needs, you'll know which one of them to look for. For example, if you want inspiring stories about faith, you'll read about Jesus Christ. If you're looking for topics about freedom, you'll remember Martin Luther King. If you need advice about your finances, Brian Tracy could be your guy. And, if you need advice about women empowerment, of course, you'll read Oprah Winfrey's works.

But they're not the only people who can make an impact on this world. I believe that all of us can. Sometimes, you may not know how to speak out, might be afraid, or you don't know the right words to say. Have you ever presented in school or at work and felt as if you were not effective enough for people to remember what you've just said? Despite the scripts and the visual aids, it seems as if people keep dozing off no matter how much you try to gather their attention. What if that presentation could have been your big break? What if your grades or promotion depended on it? Wouldn't it be great to have the skill and knowledge to present effectively? This way, you'll know that you have a better chance of achieving your goals. Bothersome, isn't it? Believe it or not, this happens to most people. It's not that they're not prepared or they lack the resources. It's just they haven't exercised their power of effective communication. Much like bodybuilding, communication is a muscle that needs to be toned to become an effective communicator. This does not only mean practicing over and over. It also means practicing the correct routine so you can use it efficiently.

We have seen many people fail in retaining the attention of their audience. While their topics are interesting and their words are inspiring, they cannot get people pay attention and remember. Most people come in strong, full of passion, and hope to inspire people only to feel demotivated because nobody seems to be listening. After a few minutes in, you can already see people doodling, chatting, and using their phones. It's as if they can't wait for your communication to be over.

The problem, my friend, is not your topic. The problem is your ability to retain the interest of your audience from your first word to your last. That's one of the greatest issues of people in public speaking and it's one that we need to solve. How? Here are some of the most recommended ways:

1. Know Your Subject

One of the primary ways to keep your audience interested is to show them that you are reliable and knowledgeable. When a speaker doesn't know his or her subject or topic, it will always show. The audience will notice that the speaker is just guessing what to say next or is not sure about what he or she is saying. This is one of the main reasons people lose interest. They don't want to listen to someone who seems unreliable and inconsistent. If the audience feels like you are wasting their time, they will most likely leave or do something else instead of listening to you.

By knowing your topic from within, your audience will notice your passion. By doing ample research and knowing your topic by heart, knowledge will come naturally even if you forget your script or if you take sudden questions. Also, it doesn't hurt if you read about related topics. This way, you can make links and provide brief explanations in case your audience asks about it.

2. Connect to Your Audience

One of the greatest ways to captivate your audience from the start is by building your rapport. This means making them feel as if you belong with them, and that they can relate to you. It's important that you make them feel special, by making the topic about them or something they know about. This entails knowing your audience aside from your topic. One of the things you will learn in communication and public speaking classes is to always know your audience. Never forget to ask about their culture, age group, status, career, and other possible information you can use. This way, you can tailor your spiels and stories in a way your audience can relate.

Can you imagine making jokes about bills to a bunch of teenagers? Or making jokes about the stock market at a wedding? Of course, your audience cannot relate. There will be a lot of dead air and awkward stares. This is why you need to know the culture of the majority of your audience so you can adjust based on their preferences.

3. Maintain Eye Contact

William Shakespeare once said that our eyes are the windows to the soul. This is where people show their true intent, their true nature. This is why we trust people when they make eye contact with us. When people cannot look you directly in the eye, you may think that something is wrong or that they are not telling the truth. The same is true for communicating and public speaking. People who make eye contact with the crowd are more likely to catch their attention. This is because you're making the audience feel like the message is really for them and that they need to listen. It also shows them how passionate and confident you are in your subject.

You might ask, "How often should I make eye contact with my audience?" Well, whatever you do, do not stare for more than five seconds at only one individual, or else, you might scare them. Try to look at other areas every once in a while, so everyone feels like they belong.

While doing so, try to look at their reactions to what you are saying. This will give you a hint on what to do next. If your audience seems confused, clarify something or ask the group if they have any questions. If your audience looks bored, come up with an icebreaker to redirect their attention towards you. If they are affirming what you are saying by nodding or smiling, it means they can relate or they're trying to absorb what you're telling them.

So, you see, making eye contact is vital. It will not only show your credibility and reliability but it will also tell you what to do next to captivate the crowd.

4. Ask Questions

The next technique that most professional orators recommend is asking questions. This is a great way to pique the minds of your audience. It wakes them up and allows them to pay closer attention to you. Whether it is a rhetorical question or dialectic, open-ended or close-ended, this method is effective to keep the audience's mind focused.

This is why we often hear public speakers ask questions every once in a while. It may be about the audience's perspective, their experiences, and many more. Even though most won't get to share it with the crowd, they will answer the question in their minds, making them more interested in other answers. In some cases where the topic is controversial, people may be open to debating one another, which is an effective way to keep them focused on the answers you are going to give.

For example, say your communication is about budgeting in finance. One way to hook your audience is by asking them how they budget their salary every month. Of course, different answers will emerge, allowing people to decide whether these are great ideas. They will then be interested in the best technique that you, as the speaker will recommend.

5. Storytelling

From the list of inspiring people at the beginning of the chapter, whom do you think is the most famous? Of course, Jesus Christ! He's known on every continent! Although he's not known for his storytelling techniques, he became famous because of the stories told about him and his miracles. Many children already know about Jesus Christ by the time they're three and these stories get remembered until they're old. This is because children are able to visualize and imagine as the story was told, allowing them to retain more information, even if it was unrelated to the story.

Storytelling, I believe, is the most effective strategy to becoming an effective speaker. This will not only help your audience focus but it will also help them remember the concepts for a long time. This method allows speakers to clearly illustrate the topic in a way that people can conceptualize the main idea. Much like telling stories, there is an exposition, a rising action, a climax, falling action, and a conclusion. This makes your audience listen from the very beginning to the end while absorbing what you say.

Can you imagine if Jesus Christ was introduced to us in an unstructured way?

"Jesus is the son of Mary and Joseph. He was born in Bethlehem. He grew up to be man's savior. He was miraculous."

Try reading this to your child and look at his or her reaction. I can almost guarantee that you will see disinterest. In a matter of minutes, your child will forget who Jesus is, because the method of communication is not interesting enough to absorb. There is no structure, it's merely stating sentences. So, let's try a different approach.

"One day, Mary received a message from an angel of God. He said 'Mary, my name is Gabriel. I have brought a very important message."

Mary had never seen an angel before so she was afraid. But the angel said, 'Don't worry Mary, I will not hurt you; the angel continued, 'you will be giving birth to the Son of God, and you will name him Jesus. He will be the savior of humankind."

See, now even you are more interested in reading the rest of the story. This technique does not only apply to children, but all ages. This is because everybody can use their imagination. Minds will fill in the gaps in the story to make it look realistic and worth remembering. So, even if you're not interested at all, your mind will lay out the scenario. You'll be surprised by the details you can remember because every little detail is vital to make the story complete in your head.

Effective, Don't You Think?

However, storytelling does not only entail telling the first story that comes to your mind. It's far from that. There is a process you need to follow to make sure the story is timely and related to your topic. It should be a part of the preparation, not just an adlib that you can include from time to time. This is the reason why you need to create a structure. This may include the following parts:

1. Explaining the problem. To entice your listeners, explaining the current situation is a good approach. This makes them realize that there really is a problem and it needs to be solved immediately.
2. Why people should listen. Let them know that they can benefit from your speech or idea. Emphasize that they can learn something that they can apply to make the situation better.
3. Causes of the problem. At this stage, let them know the root cause of the problem. You can present statistical data or research. Better yet, you can use a story that will keep them interested in your topic.
4. Possible solutions. The next step is to tell your audience the possible solutions to the problem. What can they do to solve it? What are the pros and cons of each solution?
5. Chosen solutions. Lastly, let them know which of the solutions you suggested is the best. Here, you can emphasize the reason you picked it by telling a story or showing more data that will convince people of the effectiveness of this plan.

This can serve as the backbone of your communication to make sure the speech is organized, relatable, and interesting. By following this guide, you can effectively pitch in your stories, to make them seem natural, timely, and stimulating. How do you do that? Let's look at one of the most recommended ways to structure your speech, presentation, spiel, or written output.

Section 2: The Pyramid Principle

Structured communication comes from structured thinking. This is a technique that allows speakers to effectively communicate their topic. At the same time, it makes them look confident and reliable.

This can grab the attention of the audience from the get-go. From the moment you speak your first word, your audience will lend you their ears for the rest of your presentation. Even if they have a short attention span, your ability to lift their mood and pique their mind with your structure and words will make them want more. So how do people have structured thinking? One way is to use the Pyramid Principle. Coined by Barbara Minto in the 1970s, it shapes how people structure and solve problems efficiently. This principle is a revolutionary way to share ideas.

As the name implies, it starts with the main idea, and then it gets broken down as you go. What do you need to do?

1. Start by giving the core message of your speech.

Always lead with the **assertion**, also known as the key takeaway of your speech. This is the main idea or the answer to the main question. It should be clear and concise to hook your audience. One way to make sure that you deliver your point is to use the SCQ framework: Situation, Complication, and Question.

• Situation: What is happening right now? Make sure that the audience can relate to the current situation.

- Complication: What's the problem? Deliver this in a sense that the audience will be motivated to listen because there is a sense of urgency.
- Question: This follows the complication to start the question-and-answer flow.

Finally, you will give the solution and go down the pyramid.

2. Show your supporting arguments.

This will then lead you to "Why?" This is where you logically group and summarize the supporting details as to why you chose that answer. Most experts recommend having three to seven supporting arguments for every main idea. Three is often better. This will allow your audience to easily remember the concepts. Here are good examples of using a triad:

- Three R's of waste disposal: Reduce, Reuse, and Recycle.
- The Business Triad: Business Case, People/Politics, and Project Management.
- The Epidemiological Triad: Agent, Host, and Environment.

Even if you're not a businessman or a scientist, you can easily remember the concepts above because it's simplified into three. You can do the same when you're trying to prove your point. If possible, structure it so people can easily come up with an acronym. This way, the chance of retention is higher.

3. Lastly, lay down your supporting facts.

Your supporting facts are the legwork of your main arguments. This is where you add more details about each of the supporting arguments. You could use actual figures, research data, statistics, or even testimonials that will support the arguments.

Remember, the key to having an effective structure is simplicity. Make sure your audience will understand the data you present to them. No matter how great the data you present is, it invalidates the purpose of effective communication if they cannot understand it. Therefore, you need to simplify your arguments and facts in a way that they can be relatable and worth remembering.

To help you simplify your pyramid, you can use the 7Cs of effective communication coined by Cutlip and Center in 1952. According to them, your message should be:

- Clear—easy to understand.
- Concise—avoid redundant words.
- Concrete—backed by credible data.
- Complete—information should be relevant.
- Correct—grammatically correct.
- Coherent—the arguments should be connected to the core message.
- Courteous—the method of speaking is friendly without a hint of passive aggressiveness or hostility.

Being courteous is supported by Albert Merahbin's concept of communication. He said that 90% of communication is not what you say, it's how you say it. Your audience will sense even the slightest undertone, so you need to rehearse before you present. You could try recording yourself and see how you come across. You can also ask for the help of some friends and family so they can give honest feedback about your tone and manner of speaking.

It doesn't end there. There are other factors you need to consider when using the Pyramid Principle. This includes your audience's culture, your topic, and your location. So, how can you tailor your pyramid to every scenario? Read on to the next chapter for the seven effective ways to structure your story.

Section 3: Ways to Structure Your Story

Now that you know the backbone of storytelling, you may be wondering, "Will the Pyramid Principle work in all scenarios?" It depends. Of course, you need to consider the culture of your audience—their age and background. You also need to consider the topic of your presentation. Tailor your speech into something that your audience can easily grasp and understand. Depending on the background of your audience and your situation, here are seven ways you can structure your story:

1. The Situation-Complication-Resolution Cycle

If you aim to persuade your audience, this structure is the best for you. It allows you to introduce the problems that society is facing today, and the problems that we may be facing, so you can introduce an efficient solution. Allow them to visualize the current situation so they can imagine the effects if people don't act now. To make your presentation more intriguing, you can add real-life examples, credible data, and facts.

In summary, using the Situation-Complication-Resolution cycle entails you to follow this format:
• Situation: What is happening right now?
• Complication: What is the problem?
• Resolution: What is the solution?

2. Hook, Meat, Payoff

This next structure is ideal for people who want to relay information to their audience. Usually, when people give informative speeches, many of their audience members get bored because of their inability to retain their attention. To avoid this problem, use Hook, Meat, and Payoff.

This structure allows you to pique the curiosity of the audience, giving them the motivation to listen until the end of your speech. It gives them the impression that there's a need to finish the presentation to get what I need. This usually answers the question, "What's in it for me?" So, how do you do it? The answer is a three-step process: Hook, Meat, and Payoff.

The beginning of your speech should include the hook where you develop your audience's interest in the topic. In this stage, you need to give them a strong reason why they need to listen. Do they need this to further their career? Do they need this to get good grades?

The next step is giving the meat. This is where you make them understand the topic. In the Pyramid Principle, this is where you give them the arguments and the facts supporting it.

Last is the payoff. Let your audience know that they can benefit from what they have learned. You can cite different examples of how to apply it so they can get what they have been promised at the beginning.

This structure is usually used by Simon Sinek, specifically when he talked about "How Great Leaders Inspire Action." If you listen to his approach, he started with a question that would hook the listeners, making them curious about the topic. He used questions to pique the audience's minds, grasping their attention. Once he knew that the audience is all ears, he started to present his argument. In the end, Sinek explained how the audience can benefit from the main idea, which made them want to apply the concepts they learned.

3. Situation-Opportunity-Resolution

This is a variation to the first structure we discussed in this chapter. It is better suited when you are trying to inform people about alternatives and opportunities that people can opt for. With this structure, your goal is to let the audience know the current situation and then give them alternatives that can lead to a better outcome. After you have proposed the alternatives and opportunities, you will then choose the best solution and present the facts that support it. This is effective in driving people to believe and act on the current problem that they're facing.

4. The Pitch

This structure is perfect for giving sales presentations. It makes the audience believe that your idea can help them solve a problem. Here's what the structure looks like:

- The Wind Up—This phase includes the current scenario.
- The Hurdle—Refers to the problem that needs to be solved.
- The Vision—In this phase, give the audience a glimpse of how the problem can be solved.
- The Options—Illustrate two options that can solve the problem.
- The Close—Share the best option for the problem.
- The Fine Print—Emphasize how the solution can solve the problem.
- The Hook—Lastly, showcase the benefits of applying the solution.

Using this method, you can use case studies, researchers, testimonials, and experiments to back your arguments. A good example would be how Enric Sanla presented how people can turn the high seas into the largest nature reserve. By using the pitch structure, he was able to make people aware of what they can contribute to their country.

5. The Explanation

The next structure is ideal for educating people using information-rich presentations. This method progresses in an upward direction, starting by depicting the current situation and explaining where we need to be or what we need to attain. In this process, the speaker needs to ensure that the audience understands how and why each stage can affect them. In the end, the speaker would explain the final transformation or the end goal. To summarize this approach, here are the steps you need to follow:

- The Lay of the Land—This is where you depict the current situation.
- The Roadmap—This shows the audience how to reach the final destination.
- The First Step—This is the first step that the audience needs to make to achieve the goal.
- The Next Step—Include further steps to achieve the end goal.
- Almost There—Emphasize how much your listeners have progressed since the first step.
- The Arrival—Lastly, indicate the end of the journey and what the audience will benefit from the steps you laid out on the road map.

Using this process, many speakers are afraid they might bore the audience with lots of information. The caveat of this process goes back to simplicity. Make sure you present as concisely and simply as possible so you can avoid bombarding your audience with boring details. Keep them listening by making sure that they can relate. Ask them questions, maintain eye contact, and use appealing visual aids to help your audience understand what you are saying.

6. Fact and Storytelling

This is effective in communicating a vision so the audience can feel inspired to attain the goal. This approach entails a zigzag pattern instead of a linear one. It starts with "how things worked then" and ends with "what could be" to give momentum to your presentation. This keeps your listeners at the edge of their seats because they're waiting for better solutions and processes for improvement.

Much like writing a play, this method of fact and storytelling is threefold: We have the Beginning Act, the Middle Act, and the End.

- The Beginning Act—In this phase, paint the picture of the reality that your audience is experiencing today and then add your vision. This will serve as your call to adventure, making your audience realize that there's room for improvement and that there are ways to accomplish it.
- The Middle Act—Once you have laid down the current situation, present the contrasting content. Include specific scenarios today and follow up with an alternative reality if they do a specific task. Have at least three scenarios that cause problems and let your audience know what could happen if they take action.
- The End—If everything goes smoothly, your audience will leave the room motivated to take action. They may not remember the exact words you said during the presentation, but they will be left with the vision that you depicted for them. This is enough to inspire them to take action.

7. The Drama

This next structure is effective for inspirational speeches. It allows people to live through the story through your words, making it more effective in making people remember the lesson. The eight steps of the drama structure are as follows:

- One Fine Day—This is the situation that the main character is in.
- The Challenge—This is the problem that the main character needs to face.

- Descending Crisis—In this stage, something happens that makes the challenge more difficult.
- Rock Bottom—Everything is at its worst for the hero.
- The Discovery—The hero sees a light at the end of the tunnel, a ray of sunshine, that will give him or her hope.
- The Rise—This is the phase where the hero starts to solve the problem.
- The Return—The hero overcomes the challenge.
- The Lesson—This is where you give the audience the key takeaway from the story.

When using the drama structure, make sure that the audience can relate to the story. It should be related to the main point of your presentation. Compared to other structures, here's where you can elaborate on some parts of the story, especially if it adds flare or interest to the picture you are depicting. Tell the story in such a way that the audience can live through it, so they can imagine the scenario and remember the lessons they gather.

Based on experience, this is the most used structure in presentations. You can use this anywhere—be it finance topics, business meetings, or delivering your sales pitch. You can always add a story somewhere in your presentation so your listeners can learn a lesson.

By telling stories, you leave the room with your audience motivated because this method allows you to evoke emotions that will make the concepts worth remembering. As Maya Angelou once said, people may not remember everything you say, but they will remember what you made them feel—be it sadness, happiness, anger, or disappointment. Your audience will remember you and the lesson you taught by just remembering how they felt at that moment.

Now, we already know that there are seven ways to organize your communication. But did you know that there are several other ways to do it depending again on your audience and your topic? Now, let's look at additional five storytelling frameworks that will help you create a structured and interesting storyline.

Section 4: Story Frameworks for Better Storytelling

Everybody wants to tell their story. However, not everyone can tell it efficiently. Some are at a loss for words while most do not know how to structure their stories in such a way that their audience can understand. Some of you may wonder, "How come my friends don't remember my stories? Every time I see them, I have to tell the same story over again." It's not that your story is uninteresting. Rather, this may be caused by a lack of structure. You may be jumbling the events, confusing your listeners, and making them unable to remember the details of your story.

That ends now. By understanding how you can further structure, you can tell your stories in such a way that your audience can visualize, understand, and remember. So, the next time you see your friends, they're not going to ask for the same story, they're going to ask for the sequel. You will make them come back for more.

Without further ado, here are five effective ways to structure your story.

1. Freytag's Pyramid: Five-Act Structure
Gustav Freytag, a German author, conducted a study in 1863 about the dramatic structure of popular plays. He found that a story should have five parts to entice the audience:

- Exposition—This is where you introduce the story, giving the audience the beginning scene where the story starts.
- Rising Action—This stage consists of a series of events that build up to the climax.
- Climax—Refers to the most exciting part of the story.
- Falling Action—After the climax, this phase is where the protagonist solves the problem and learns his lesson.
- Denouement—The end of the story. This comes with the resolution and revelation of the play.

You can see countless brand ambassadors use this format. A good example would be The Charity Water Story where they used humanized brand storytelling.

2. The Three-Act Structure

This is a shorter version of the five-act dramatic structure. This is commonly used in social media postings where readers and listeners opt for short advertisements. Compared to the five-act structure, this is more straightforward, focusing more on introducing the concept or could be a brand rather than adding details to the story. The three-act structure consists of the following parts:

- The setup—This is where you set the scene and introduce the characters.
- Rising action—Also known as the confrontation, is where you present the problem or the tension build-up.
- The resolution—Refers to the blissful ending and resolution of the problem presented.

3. The StoryBrand Framework

This method coined by Donald Miller is a great way to make the audience imagine as if they are the protagonist of the story. It is based on the narrative structure of Joseph Campbell's "hero's journey," which helps brands create a memorable story arc. It allows the audience to relate to the story and message, enticing them to buy the message. The structure is as follows:

- A character—The speaker will create a character that allows the audience to relate to his perspectives and personality. This is why you need to do some digging about the people listening to you during the presentation.
- The problem—Refers to the difficulty that the main character will face, preferably one that the audience is facing in reality.
- The guide—The hero meets a guide. In this case, it will be you as the speaker.
- The plan—You will then give them a plan of action they can use.
- The call to action—You will motivate them to act now to solve the problem.
- Success or Failure—When they take action, explain how they can benefit from the solution. If they don't, explain the detrimental effects.

4. The Pixar Story Framework

Another effective way to tell stories is the Pixar Story Framework. This method goes beyond solutions and ideas because it touches people and makes them emotional. It makes us remember the lessons for a long time. Emma Coates from Pixar created this framework when she was telling stories for Pixar. You may already know some of the most legendary movies they produced like Cars, Inside Out, Onward, and Coco, not to mention Toy Story and the Incredibles. All of them are amazing movies because of the format they use to tell stories. The Pixar Story Framework relies on six phrases that the storyteller will finish:

- Once upon a time, _____

This involves the background of your story.

- Every day, _____

Add supporting details that would describe your story setting.

- Then one day, _____

This introduces the conflict and its cause.

- Because of that, _____

Add the challenge that the hero will face.

- And because of that, _____

Include supporting details to the problem like how it affected the character, and who else are affected?

- Until finally, _____

This is the light at the end of the tunnel on how the hero would solve the problem, leading to the ending of the story.

Who knows, you may be creating one of the best stories of all time.

5. Features and Benefits Formula

This formula created by Harry Dry is one of the most effective storytelling structures. It allows the speaker to emphasize the features and benefits of the solutions and pitches easily. This formula serves as an amazing entry point because it allows you to create a richer story that will entice your audience.

The formula is as follows:
- Describe the Solution.
- So what? What does the audience get from it?
- Compare the old way and follow up with the effects of using the solution you recommend.
- Emphasize how the listeners can use the solution.

Section 5: The End

There you have it! These are some of the most effective ways to structure your communication and come up with an amazing story that will interest your audience. Although it's hard to practice, you shouldn't lose hope. No one is born a natural speaker. The difference between amazing orators and typical ones, however, is that they never cease to learn and practice. You should do the same. Whenever you need to communicate something important, use these structures based on the nature of your audience and your topic. Then, try to rehearse in front of family or friends, record yourself, or practice in front of a mirror. This way, you can determine what needs to be improved.

You can choose from the different structures we discussed, depending on your topic and audience. What matters most is you deliver your communication as simply and concisely as possible, in a way that your audience will apply and remember.

How to Access Your Bonuses

With this book, **you also get access to:**

a) **Our Q&A premium service,** ask us any question on any topic contained in the book, or on the application of the concepts to your own situations, problems, and opportunities.

b) **The ebooklet "System Thinking Principles"**

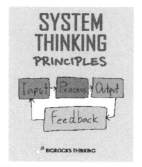

Scan the QR code below to get access:

Or got to:

https://bigrocksgroup.com/thinkingunlimited

In addition, we give several free consultation sessions every month, you may get lucky and get also a free 30-minutes consultation session with one of our consultants. Insert the codeword "Free Session" at the end of your message.

How Can You Get the Best Out of This Book

This book gives you a theoretical and practical preparation to help you understand the key pillars of Critical Thinking, Logic and Problem Solving. To get the maximum benefits out of this guide we recommend the followings:

1) Use mind maps to absorb well the key concepts
2) Use memory techniques such as Memory Palace to retain the key info
3) Practice, Practice, Practice
4) Adopt the Feynman technique and try to educate with what you have learned someone unaware of the topic.

Made in United States
North Haven, CT
22 April 2023

35701646R00063